IN THE LIGHT OF

A JOURNEY OF TRANSFORMATION

Published by

Librario Publishing Ltd

ISBN: 1-904440-22-3

Copies can be ordered via the Internet
www.librario.com

or from:

Brough House, Milton Brodie, Kinloss
Moray IV36 2UA
Tel /Fax No 00 44 (0)1343 850 617

IN THE LIGHT OF THE RAINBOW TREE

A JOURNEY OF TRANSFORMATION

By Susie Rose Alexander

Librario

Introduction

The woman in the sunny box is the narrator of Susie's story. She sees it in the light of the Rainbow Tree Project, a huge textile exhibition, made over a seven-year period, by hundreds of children from all over the world, which serves as the vehicle for her journey of transformation.

The story starts when wee Susie was seven years old.

The child had a catastrophic fall down stairs resulting in her being treated as an invalid for eighteen months. She was shut up on the top floor of the Edinburgh house, in which she was born, with only her Nannie for company. Susie did not know what was wrong with her but believed that her inner light had gone out and that she has lost the key to her whole life.

When she was sent back to school, at the age of nine, Susie felt hopelessly out of place. It was a talent for ballet dancing that gave her the life-line onto which she would cling until she was seven times seven years old. As a teenager, she went to a vocational boarding school in England, subsequently joining the Royal Ballet in 1954. For the next seven years Susie led an exciting life of fame and travel.

In 1960 the ballerina gave up her career to marry, but she was totally unprepared for housewifery and motherhood. After the birth of her second child, a new career of teaching restored her confidence and compensated for feelings of inadequacy.

The upwardly mobile family of four thrived and enjoyed happy summers in their holiday home, an old water mill, on the Isle of Wight until, in 1973, the husband's firm was taken over.

The family moved to the Isle of Wight where he set up his own business in the water mill. Once again Susie found herself out of her depth. She had to give up her London ballet school and now that both the children were at boarding school she felt lost. The change of circumstances put a crippling strain upon the marriage. Both husband and wife retreated into their work. He built up a milling business and she created another ballet school and a Youth Dance Company.

In 1985 Susie's health broke down. Her condition deteriorated and in February 1986 she was taken into hospital for tests. Instead of the 'death sentence' she expected, (even hoped for), she had a dramatic spiritual experience that set her on course for a journey of transformation.

She spent the following eighteen months confined, like wee Susie, to the house. Her faith grew and strengthened in an intense and unconventional way but the gulf between husband and wife deepened.

As soon as the invalid was able she went home to Scotland. Her elderly mother had recently moved to a home in Perthshire and Susie hoped to buy a cottage nearby.

When her plan did not materialise, the energy of despair motivated the still frail woman to follow in her daughter's footsteps and go to India.

It was an experience that changed her whole life. She was profoundly impressed by the zest for life in materially poor and often physically disabled people, but it was a visit to a Creativity Centre for deprived children that re-ignited the light that wee Susie had lost.

One year later, on October 4, 1989, Susie left the Isle of Wight for good. It was not for a peaceful life in Scotland but to do voluntary work in a school for Bangladeshi children in London's East End. She was still unfit for paid employment so was forced to live on Income Support until she was eligible for a State pension in 1995.

New creative outlets in hand spinning, textile art and liturgical dance revealed hidden talents. Susie made a series of 'visionary altar hangings' for St. James' Church Piccadilly, became the craft worker for the Iona Community and, above all, developed her interest in children.

In September 1993 the idea of The Rainbow Tree project inspired

Susie to design and set up a vast patchwork to be made in five sections by children in India, Tower Hamlets and the Isles of Dogs, Wight and Iona. In June 1994 two children from each branch came to London to assemble the Rainbow Tree at the first live-in Festival of Friendship.

The enthusiastic response encouraged Susie to take the Rainbow Tree on a mission of friendship to Poland, Germany, the Czech Republic and Russia. Soon she realised that this was just the beginning of a far greater venture and a new vision came to the former choreographer. Every year, for seven years, two new patchworks, each linked to a colour of the rainbow and depicting shared themes of the environment and creation, would be made. This would create a vehicle to link children across the globe and produce a fantastic exhibition for the new millennium.

In the year two thousand that dream came true. It was labour of love throughout, funded only by the faith of one woman and inspired by her passionate belief in the right of the universal child to grow up in hope. The Rainbow Tree gave Susie a new sense of purpose and provided a structure upon which to rebuild her life. She travelled far and wide before her journey finally brought her home to Scotland.

The textile exhibition culminated in Russia at Easter 2001. Susie's task was completed and her journey of transformation has brought her to her true destination.

Now the narrator in the sunny box has gone and I am here. I am at home with myself in the cottage that was waiting for me in the beginning. I have discovered a deep contentment that rests, not in having much but in coveting little. I am simply living my life simply, in the light of the Rainbow Tree.

Chapter One

IN AND OUT OF THE SUNNY BOX

The woman sits in her box. The sunny box she calls it. The door of the porch is wide open. It is the first sparkling morning of the year. Deeply she breathes in the scent of the awakening earth. Beetles stretch and scurry in spring urgency across the cracking soil. Smiling pansy faces welcome her back into her garden. Back home.

The Rainbow Tree is in the bag. A large canvas bag decorated with hand painted animals sits under the table. It was specially made in India for the huge patchwork that nestles inside. The colourful holdall has accompanied the woman on many journeys and the magical tree inside it is the key to the whole story of her life.

She has travelled long and far for many years. It is nearly thirteen since she started the journey to find her lost key, and over half a century since she lost it. Her light had gone out just before she lost her key so it was no wonder she could not see where she was going. It was no wonder she fell.............

One morning at school assembly, the headmistress had told the children that each one of them had a little light burning inside them. The light was the key to God's house where they would live together in Heaven when they died. Susie listened entranced. Her heart beat rapidly inside her taut little body flickering like a candle by a window.

The head went on to stress the importance of keeping your key alight by being good helpful children who obeyed their parents and teachers and always did their homework on time. The image of a key shaped light had made a profound impression on Susie, so she tried hard to achieve all these requirements.

It was not until the following Wednesday morning that she began to doubt the power of her light. She usually enjoyed the handicraft lesson and was looking forward to making the spectacle case. The instructions were simple.

'Cut two identical shapes from the given piece of felt', said Mrs Henderson, indicating the examples she had carefully prepared the night before.

Susie set to work eagerly and soon completed the first part of the exercise. Carefully placing her two pieces together she felt her first pang of dismay. They did not match.

'Trim a little bit off the bigger one and Mrs. Henderson will never notice,' thought Susie to herself.

Dismay rapidly turned to panic when she saw that her bigger piece was now smaller than her little one. On and on she snipped and trimmed but however hard she tried she could not make her two pieces match. The spectacle case was barely wide enough to hold a small ruler by the time the bell sounded. All the other children obediently put their perfectly matched pieces into neat folders and sat tidily at their desks waiting to be dismissed by Mrs. Henderson. Susie tried to hide her emaciated pieces under her crumpled gym slip, then in the commotion of snatching up satchels and the rush to line up at the door she stuffed the whole lot up her navy blue knickers and slunk past Mrs. Henderson hot with guilt, shame and fear. The fear that gripped Susie propelled her all the way home with a desperate urgency that seemed to pursue her like a thunderous shadow licking at her heels. The black shadow overtook her in the last mad dash up the garden path and it got her just before she burst in through the front door. With a final gasp of panic Susie knew it had blown her light out.

The catastrophe of the spectacle case was now magnified into the greatest disaster of her entire seven years on this earth. Her sobs were inconsolable and she was still sniffling when it was time for her 'good-nightly' visit to the hallowed ground of her parent's drawing room. That was when she fell. Fell from the top of the nursery stairs to the dark hollow hall far below.

She knew that she must be ill when she woke up in her small narrow bed to see a fire lit in the nursery grate. Susie clutched the tight white sheet around her chin staring at sinister shadows dancing on the wall but the flickering fire gave no warmth to the icy emptiness inside her stomach. No one could tell her what was wrong with her. Even the doctor did not know and could only advise complete rest for an indefinite period. No school; no friends; no spectacle cases; no orange sponge cakes. She lay lost in a vast darkness with no key to unlock her loneliness _ she, had lost her way, lost her light, and it seemed to the child that she had even lost the key to life itself.

Eighteen months later someone suddenly said, 'You're better now. You can go back to school.'

Better! Susie felt much worse. She had forgotten the language of school. She had had no one to talk to for a year and half except Ming her teddy bear. Ming was Chinese so conversation was limited. How could she understand the rules of the playground when the only game she had played was the dreaded 'Truth and Dare' on Nanny's day off when her elder sisters took charge? Week after week it was always the same, there was only one game. To Susie it was a game of torture. Like hockey. She could not think fast enough to answer the hard, hurting questions. She could not leap high enough to avoid the hard, hurtling ball. She was too small, her muscles were too weak.

The only fresh air and exercise she had taken for many months was when Nannie pushed her out in a pram as if she was a baby. The shame of it covered her still like the knitted pink shawl she hid beneath on the compulsory afternoon constitutionals. Whenever they met anyone Nannie would purse her thin lips and whisper inaudible replies to enquiries after Susie's health. The child assumed that she had something too shameful to be mentioned aloud. Back at school she felt like a stranger in an alien world. She was a misfit, though into what she was supposed to fit she never did discover even when the years told her that she was a grown up. She often felt more like a grown down. She did not know what she was meant to be a lot of the time. She only knew she was a pain. People often told her so. She certainly hurt a lot, inside and out.

But she never forgot the magical image of God's house with all the little lights of good children shining through the windows like the candle in her bedside nightlight. She clung to the belief that one day she would find her key and unlock the dream of happiness that is inborn within the innocence of every child. Her dream was shattered many times but it always grew again through the rich soil of suffering like the seed of a dying tree. The woman Susie has become sometimes feels as she herself is a like a tree growing out of the ground of her own being. It is as if she cannot become herself until she has grown into her shape, the only shape into which she can fit.

And then a strange thing happened when Susie was seven times seven years old. She fell down stairs again. Different stairs, different house, different place, different time, but she hurtled back into the place and time she had lost forty- two years ago.

Eighteen months later no one said, 'you are better now'. No one told her to go back to school. This time there was no going back. There was nowhere to go back to, nothing left except the compelling need to get up, go out into the world, and find her key.

Susie was old now. Frail and bent, walking with the aid of a fold up stick bought at the disabled department of Boots before setting out on this journey of a lifetime. She carried her childhood dream within the locked prison of her memory as she entered the doorless dilapidation of the dark building, leaving the hot dusty village outside. Cries of welcome penetrated the filigree layers of grief which shrouded her like a threadbare shawl. The fabric of her life had unravelled like an old piece of knitting, the pattern of which had been lost long ago.

Welcome,' the high voices sang out in unison. 'Come and see what we are making'

Dozens of gleaming brown eyes lit the dark room like candles in the night. Eager brown fingers wound their way round her pale papery hands pulling her into the centre of the place. The place, she had been told, was a creativity centre for poor children. She could see no poor children here except in her heart. The rich excitement, the keen delight of the sing song voices reached her again.

'Come and see, we are making a tree'

The tree rose from the ground. A small tree of newspaper spiralled upwards creating movement where there was none. Suddenly, the whole room was lit up with colour.

It was everywhere. In the worn, torn embroidery on a girl's purple dress; in the boys' indigo blue-black hair glossy with cheap oil; in the startling blue sky glimpsed through a hole in the wall and in a green plastic bag bulging with bananas and oranges. Red painted toe and fingernails jumped and clapped on calloused feet and grubby hands. A veritable rainbow seemed to infuse the drab paper tree with a surprising loveliness.

Susie's eyes gleamed with a glistening light, her inner child leapt for joy. She knew that these shabby, scraggy children recognised her from the beginning. It was as if they had all lived together in God's house from the beginning. Presenting her with the little rainbow tree the children said,

'See, here is your key, we kept it for you all these years. We knew you would come.

Welcome, well come.'

* * *

Back in the sunny box the woman ponders the mystery of the key. She had not expected to find it in such an unlikely place or such an unusual shape. A key is not much use without a door or a box or even a window. That reminds her that she has indeed lost the key to her windows. They are new to the old cottage, double glazed, draught-sealed, security proofed and unable to be opened without the key;

which she has lost. Replacing it is not a simple matter either. In fact it is impossible without the serial number of the key. And she has lost that too! She opens the porch door instead.

The cottage is stuffy and dusty. She finds sharp, shiny surfaces disturb her winter somnambulance. The woman's wandering mind settles on her key again, like the butterfly on the yellow dandelion.

'How could it possibly have found its way to India?' she asks herself. India is a long way from Scotland. Had she ever lived there in a past life, she muses.

She certainly felt as if she had when she visited a children's dancing class on her next trip there the following year. It was so different from the Saturday morning class she used to attend and later, much later, teach.

What was it about the gazelle-like bodies that made her cry? It was not the beauty of the slim brown limbs nor the grace of the sleek black haired heads, not even the poignant, pungent fragrance of freshly picked marigolds interwoven in intricately plaited coils.

No, it was the holiness. Each child solemnly made her 'puja' before the exercises began. The sacred dance was not approached without the utmost reverence, tender young bodies offered up to Shiva the dancing god with wide-eyed humility.

'Why hadn't I done that?' the child wailed within the watching woman. Why had no one told her she was entering sacred ground when her feet trod the rough, bruised planks of her dancing studio floor? Even in a cold Northern city there is holiness.

Was that what upset her so much in the latter years of her long career? Yes, she'd been successful. Yes, she'd been acclaimed as a rising star, but her star had fallen lower year by year. Now it was in free fall.

Those children, those innocents who were brought to her renowned ballet school, those little stars still sparkling with the untarnished belief in their inborn ability to dance, came to her in droves. For what? To have the heavenly gift of inner rhythm bridled into an eight-count beat? To have the natural grace of all God's creatures (from snail to thunder cloud) squashed into a uniform? A uniform that didn't fit and wasn't fitting for the originality of every created body. The ballet teacher had known then that there was something wrong in the way the syllabus seemed to crush individuality into a one sized box. 'I've yet to meet a box shaped person', she thought.

Here in India it was all so different. Another world altogether. The organic creativity channelled back to whence it came in an endless spiralling dance. Spirals are not circles. They do not go round and round. They go round and up and sometimes round and down but always round and out. They come out of themselves.

* * *

'Come out!' someone cries. 'Come out of your box'.

The woman wakes with a start. Sitting in her sunny box she lifts her eyes to the distant hill and sees that it is dancing.

Chapter Two

A PLACE OF YOUR OWN

She smiles. Everything dances for her now. It had not always been so, in fact when Susie first discovered dancing it had merely been an escape from the daily nightmare of school. She never did get the hang of long division, she failed utterly to see the point of algebra and the bewildered boredom she found hard to conceal during Latin lessons often got her into trouble. She was a puny wee thing and gained an infamous reputation for being a 'peely-wally' pain at her Edinburgh school. Puking panic attacks were dismissed as yet another example of her inability to be like other children. Bright, confident, clever she was not. It seemed there was nothing she could do right until the day something happened to change the course of her life forever.

That day they were called out of the usual Friday spelling test to go down to the gym for a very different kind of test. It was not their brains which were to be assessed but their bodies. This was a concept foreign to most of the girls, who were required to line up at the parallel bars in nothing more than their navy blue knickers and stocking feet.

The ballet teacher cast a cold calculating eye around the hall with a professional detachment that Susie was to acquire in the unforeseen future. She searched for slight, delicate physiques considered inadequate on the games field. Highly arched insteps were an added bonus, rare and exciting to find. Susie's wide- eyed pallor and nervous demeanour further caught the attention of the selector's gaze.

Three small girls were chosen to attend the weekly ballet class which the school was adding to the cultural curriculum, currently limited to Scottish country dancing and percussion.

'Wee Susie, aged 9'

Rehearsals for *Giselle*

**The author dances in the title role of *Giselle* as a soloist in the
Royal Ballet at Covent Garden**

Still dancing – Christmas in Russia, 1995

Suddenly Susie found herself plucked out of the mystifying muddles in which she seemed to become immersed week after week. Now Tuesday afternoons lit up her whole life in a way she had not experienced before. Not even the carefree years before the fated fall had contained the joy Susie felt when she danced. At last she had found something she could do, something she could do better than the few others who attempted to master the skill of executing an 'entre-chat' or a 'cabriole devant'.

Long division no longer terrorised one who could lift her leg up behind her ear or do the splits at the drop of a scornful taunt in the playground.

Dancing became a new way of life for Susie. It led her right away from Scotland to a country she had never visited before, when she was sent to a ballet school in England.

At first, the thirteen year old found it difficult to adjust, but Susie soon acquired a speaking voice that blended in with the Southern accents and made her more acceptable to her new schoolmates. Neither mathematics nor science were included in this curriculum so she didn't have to worry about algebra or equations any more. Ballet dancing was the main subject and with daily classes she rapidly progressed from 'pirouette' to 'pas-de-chat' and passed all the examinations with ease.

Soon after leaving school at the age of seventeen and much to the surprise of fellow students, teachers, parents and Susie herself, the promising young dancer was accepted into the touring company of the Royal Ballet. For the next seven years dancing was her whole world, a world within a world to which she felt she belonged at last.

Home became the small square allotted to each member of the travelling company in every dressing room of the many different theatres at which they performed week after week. This was your place. It was immensely important. Your place and everything arranged upon it was all you could claim as your own. The first thing you did each Monday morning was to lay out your place. Like a sacred ritual to start the new week, pots, brushes, powder puffs, mascots and photographs were unpacked from the regulation biscuit tin. Everyone had their own unique style. Make up jars were colour co-ordinated with plastic mat, tissues and hand towel. Even your dressing gown was chosen to match the overall effect.

After the final Saturday night performance your entire place had to be repacked into the biscuit tin and stowed in the company's travelling skip along with the pillow case provided for your practise clothes and ballet shoes.

Even when Susie became a ballerina, and had her name in lights in Johannesburg or danced the leading roles in Adelaide, Aberdeen and the Alhambra Gardens her place never outgrew the three foot square plastic mat or the ubiquitous tin.

The tightly knit family of dancers had little experience of 'normal life' except on the tedious Sunday train journeys, which inevitably involved long waits and changes at dreary stations all reminiscent of Crewe. To pass the time, the girls used to fantasise about whom they would marry, imagining that their very own Prince Charming would whisk them away to a golden castle in the sky. They were still children at heart, believing the happy ending stories they danced out on many a rough or steeply sloping stage.

No time was allowed to recover from these journeys from theatre to theatre, even on overseas tours. Whether it was a three day flight to Australia, a two week sea voyage to South Africa or a nine hour bumping bus drive across rural Spain, rehearsals commenced the morning after arrival and the first performance was usually on the same night. Your identity was dancer, your function was dancing, your purpose was to uplift, to inspire, to entertain and above all to transform the normal, the mundane into the extraordinary and amazing.

Not all the fairy tales Susie danced had happy endings. In fact her first and favourite role was a tragedy. She poured her heart into the broken heart of the rejected peasant girl, she wept real tears of anguish as she abandoned herself to the demented mind of Giselle. The intensity of her poignant grief was such that many a hardened critic found unaccustomed lumps in their throats and fumbled for forgotten handkerchiefs.

How was it that a twenty one- year-old girl could portray such passion they wondered? It was almost as if she wasn't acting and what they witnessed on the stage of the Royal Opera House was uncomfortably realistic at times.

* * *

The woman looks back into the window of her past. A soft breeze drifts through the open door of the sunny box wrapping her in a cloak of melancholy. Her premature departure from the stage still seems such a waste of so much undanced talent.

She views the collected reality of her life surrounding her now.

The garden fork propped up against an old pair of boots, the battered straw hat bought at some forgotten seaside resort and an assortment of stones brought home from the beach. She loves stones. These every day ordinary things are weaving together past tragedies, fantasies, joys and sorrows into a new pattern. All the broken threads, the unfinished lines, the dropped stitches and tangled knots are gradually being restored, like redeemed regrets. But the fabric underpinning the nostalgic woman's unknown future is still taking shape.

Another memory glides across the distant barley field to descend gracefully upon the doorstep of the sunny box. The lilting tips of slender grain evoke an image of three Swan Maidens in a faraway land. Suddenly a burst of sunshine breaks through the gloomy cloud of her reverie. The woman's mind focuses on a different stage and the years recede like an ebbing tide.

It was incredibly hot in Australia in 1958. Conditions were even more primitive in Adelaide than in Sydney, Melbourne and Brisbane. The travelling members of the Royal Ballet were not used to comfort or cosseting but the sweltering heat on that pioneering tour took them aback. Air conditioning was a luxury that did not extend beyond the auditorium therefore the dressing rooms and the stage of the King's Theatre were suffocating. There was no oxygen in the wings as there had been in airless Johannesburg and even the memory of a freezing week in Stockton-on-Tees took on a more favourable aspect, even if there was no water to wash off your make- up, at least your eyebrows had stayed in place. Here, they slid down your face in rivers of sweat, clouding your vision and putting you off balance.

Susie had been billeted in a rented suburban villa shared with three other dancers. The sultry Australian nights were no less hot than the days so they often got up in the wee, small hours to take a cold shower, creeping back to bed dripping wet in an attempt to cool off. This was done in total darkness for fear of disturbing the slumbering cockroaches lurking in every low shadowy corner and leering from tea packets in high cupboards. Every morning Susie would peel her soggy body off the sodden mattress and hurry eagerly to the rehearsal room. To enter a world where maidens flew and swans fell in love was a blessed escape from the sordid reality of the poky little house.

The great ballerina, Margot Fonteyn had flown out especially to coach Lynn Seymour and Susie in the taxing dual role of Odette/Odile in Swan Lake. This was a new addition to the repertoire of the touring company. The two soloists and their partners, Donald MacLeary and Christopher Gable were tipped as the stars of the future. Their youthful enthusiasm certainly shone with bright hopes as they learned the time- honoured roles from the most brilliant star of the British ballet world.

* * *

The vision in the woman's mind pauses like a star suspended in space. Within the invisible labyrinth of her thoughts lay the knowledge of the many performances she had given of the bewitched Swan Queen. She still carried the gift of that experience like a butterfly enfolded inside a chrysalis. She now knew that it would re-emerge, untarnished, many times through the years. But in the early years of the marriage for which she had given up her career, the former ballerina had often wondered what was the use of this hidden resource.

* * *

Susie became engaged just before the second South African tour in spring 1960 soon after her sister introduced her to a public school friend of her husband, saying,

'I've got just the man for you, Susie!'

It was high time the twenty-four and a half year old thought about settling down and raising a family like her elder siblings and the young man was eminently suitable.

It was a whirlwind romance. He swept her off her feet with candle lit dinners in expensive restaurants, bouquets of red roses and a beautiful ruby and diamond ring. He was virtually her first boyfriend. She fell in love with his dashing good looks and his persistent wooing was hard to resist.

The lure of her long held dream, 'breakfast, lunch, tea and supper' provided by a bowler-hatted businessman, complete with brief case and rolled umbrella, had never been more attractive. Her fiancé fitted the image exactly. He even had a brand new company house just waiting for a suitable wife to make it into a home. Susie seemed so sophisticated with her cultivated English accent, the perfect smoke rings she blew through a long cigarette holder and the charming way she signed numerous autographs at the stage door. But she was still a naïve young girl at heart and had little experience of the reality of worldly ways.

All through the three-months abroad she eagerly looked forward to the new life about to start soon after tour. At the end of every performance the ballerina was presented with a single red rose, wrapped in cellophane, sent by her husband-to—be. She believed marriage to be the magic wand to eternal happiness and her forthcoming role of 'The Bride' was more alluring than any other she danced. She eagerly looked forward to the day her dream would come true and she would walk up the aisle clasping a whole bouquet of red roses to the white satin folds flowing from her tiny waist.

Chapter Three

WHERE WINDOWS DO NOT WEEP

The wedding was a glamorous London affair. The bride was radiant, the groom on top form, the bridesmaids beautiful, and the guests sophisticated and smart. The reception took place in an elegant house in Hampstead and the sun shone upon the rolling lawns. The family minister travelled down from Scotland with Susie's parents to cause a sensation in the kilt and his engaging speech was given with Highland wit and lilt. The happy couple swept off on a honeymoon on Corsica, booked by the husband's secretary. It all appeared to be perfect except for one thing that had been quite overlooked.

The bride was totally unprepared for marriage. She had no idea how to be a wife.

She had not attended Domestic Science College like her elder sisters, so had no idea how to iron a man's shirt, make a bed with neat envelope corners or lay a luncheon table correctly. The cookery course that she had hastily joined a few weeks before the wedding did not prepare her for frying eggs or mashing potatoes and Duck a l'Orange with flower cut tomatoes were hardly appropriate for breakfast.

Dinner party conversation was a further hazard. It might have been advisable to sit, meekly listening, in wifely manner, but Susie was not used to filling in the background. She swotted up on current affairs by jotting down other people's opinions from radio programmes and then would throw a remark about the Common Market, or suchlike, into the social arena with what she hoped was casual aplomb. Occasionally she scored an unexpected success, like the "intercourse cigarette" she proposed between the beef stroganoff and the orange soufflé. To the sexually liberated sixties' crowd Susie's unintended pun was daringly amusing.

She was less successful on other occasions.

Winning the prize for the can-can at the Bowl's Club dinner instead of presenting it graciously from the director's table was too warmly applauded by the wrong people. Leading the entire confederation of European business men in an undignified conga round the Viennese congress hall was something that even Susie regretted the following morning.

The housewife's role was no easier to grasp than that of the social hostess. The Director's house seemed spotless, and anyway he had a woman to come in to polish the parquet floors and clean his shoes. There was little left for Susie to do except flick a feather duster around the ornaments on the mock Regency mantelpiece and between the lyre legs of the reproduction coffee tables. This she did with flair and flourish to recordings of Beatles' pop music thus liberating her disciplined dancer's limbs in new and exciting ways. But when the music stopped an icy emptiness crept into Susie's stomach reminding her of a distant lonely bed she thought she had vacated long ago.

The emptiness was filled when she became pregnant. The young wife looked forward too eagerly to motherhood. The vision of a new role swelled her imagination with the plump ripeness of her expectant belly. In her mind she choreographed the ideal mother who would have climbed to the top of the stairs to cradle away her child's nightmares in crooning arms. She imagined the baby sucking contentedly at her swelling breasts. She fantasised further into a marital bliss she still hoped to experience when the bud of their love blossomed like the rose her husband laid on her heaving belly just before she disappeared into the early labour area.

But it seemed once again that she did not know the steps of her new part, could not keep time with the unfamiliar music of the maternal instinct she so desperately longed to achieve. Susie wanted to have her baby naturally and had attended classes during pregnancy. She was confident her strong and well trained body could manage the birth without drugs but the hospital staff took no notice of her protests and stuck a needle into her arm, 'to make her have a good night's sleep before baby came.'

But baby started to come while her mother was still sedated and so could do little to help her premature child into the world.

Cross voices remonstrated with Susie even before the tiny screaming purple-faced bundle was severed from the umbilical chord. Too heavily drugged, she had failed to obey the doctor's commands to pant or push or not to push according to his directions. Hard hands pummelled her inadequate ballet dancer's breasts in unsuccessful attempts to force a reluctant dribble of milk from her tight neat nipples. The baby's frantic screams of hunger and her mother's sobs of despair failed to win sympathy from big busted nurses who bustled their annoyance for one who could not comply with the strict maternity ward routine.

By the time Susie and her shrunken baby returned to the parquet-floored house they were both swaddled in desolate dejection. It was several months before either of them recovered from the shock, but the little girl grew into a being of light who was to inspire her mother to follow in her footsteps a quarter of a century later. From the beginning her strength of character had shone through, like the copper glints in her curly hair, and had helped her triumph over her difficult entry into the world.

* * *

The woman looks back in compassion for herself. Her box is not sunny to-day.

Rain courses down the nine windowpanes like tears as she remembers the nine months pregnant with such hope and bright

25

excitement. A sense of deep disappointment seeps through the grey glass of time unhealed by the years.

Her inner dance is a lament. Emotions interweave with memory as her heart reaches out to touch the child she grew out of and the child she gave birth to and the mother she yearned to be. She longs to gather all three into a place where windows do not weep.

* * *

The birth of her second baby was quite different. It was the most joyful experience of Susie's life. It was not until years later she wondered what it had been like for him. Her son. Perhaps the speed of his headlong entry into the neon light, bright world had been a shock to one who had been cocooned in watery darkness for the past eight and a half months? The two-hour drug free roller coaster experience was a true labour of love for his mother. She loved the rapid rhythm of her body and she felt as if the baby responded like a dancing partner. She remembered how he had leapt in her womb when she was attending a concert a few weeks before. His sense of timing was certainly breath taking. He was a born musician and the dedication he was to devote to his inborn talent helped his mother to be true to hers when her body could no longer dance. Susie did not attempt to breast feed her baby boy. She just added this to the growing the list of things she couldn't do, and put him straight onto a bottle.

By now the nervous mother had come to an arrangement with the cleaning lady, Milly. She had had eight children of her own and knew far more about babies than Susie could ever hope to learn. The older woman's husband had recently died and the role of nursemaid gave new meaning to her life during bereavement.

While her little daughter and tiny son were being expertly bathed and comfortably settled with practised ease, Susie determined to scrub away her sense of failure and inadequacy by attacking the kitchen floor. This she did with feverish gusto hoping her husband would notice an impressive result.

He noticed: a small frown tightened his brow as he saw the black marks his shoes had made on the floor. Susie's stomach contracted with the same apprehension she had felt when she had neatly pruned out all next year's growth from the gooseberry bush, and the time his dinner shirt had emerged a pale shade of pink from the washing machine. The words she dreaded to hear fell into the taught silence. Staring at the vinyl tiles, now denuded of their protective polish, he sighed, 'Let's face it, darling, you're only good at one thing.'

Unwittingly, he had plunged his new wife right back into the fear of the puking child before she had discovered what her 'one thing' was. He went on encouragingly,

'Why don't you get yourself a little job at the Royal Ballet School?'

Screwing her panic up like a pocket handkerchief, she decided to take up his well meaning suggestion and approached her former boss, Dame Ninette de Valois.

It so happened that a new repertoire class had been introduced into the curriculum of the junior school at White Lodge in Richmond Park not far from their house. The recently retired ballerina was perfectly suited to teach the roles she had danced to budding stars of the future and she approached her new job with enthusiasm.

Immediately a renewed sense of purpose uplifted her flagging spirits and throughout the following two years Susie gained confidence as a ballet teacher. This eventually led to the setting up of her own school in a local church hall. 1968 was an excellent time to embark on such a venture as the Royal Academy of Dancing had just invited Dame Margot Fonteyn to devise a brand new children's examination syllabus. A golden opportunity presented itself to Susie. She could be one of the few privileged teachers to learn the work from the great lady who had taught her the graceful movements of the Swan Queen not so long ago. Once again fate had stepped in and rescued her with the life-line of dance.

The next five years were the happiest of the entire marriage. The babies grew into children who could be played with and enjoyed more easily than in the anxious early years, the Susan Alexander School of Dancing flourished, her husband was promoted to production director and bought a holiday house on the Isle of Wight for his family to relax away from the pressures of London life. It was an old water mill in an idyllic rural position a few miles from both the sea and a peaceful river estuary. London friends and Scottish relations brought their children to romp on the beach with Susie's daughter and son and the sleepy little island was popular with sailing friends who often enjoyed the wonderful parties for which her husband became renowned. They 'had never had it so good' and there was barely a cloud to be seen on the horizon of the upwardly mobile little family. Their course seemed to be set fair.

But just when Susie thought she was getting the hang of things at last, the winds of change blew a cold shadow over their charmed existence.

Chapter Four

THE KINGDOM OF DANCE

On April 1, 1973 Susie and her husband and two young children locked the door of the parquet-floored house behind them for the last time. They were leaving the comfortable life and financial security of the past thirteen years and facing a very different kind of future. The company, for whom her husband had so successfully worked, had been taken over. He had been at the forefront of the prolonged and bitter battle and was reluctant to serve under the new regime. Now with the experience and enthusiasm to set up his own business, he decided to get the old water mill on the Isle of Wight working again. Susie visualised a scene of rustic simplicity and characteristically began to choreograph a new role into which she imagined she could fit. She had not yet learnt the danger of building up unrealistic hopes and her attempts to transform herself into a humble miller's wife were singularly unsuccessful.

The husband's vision was quite different. He took his responsibilities for his family very seriously and was determined to give his children the best education he could afford. It was imperative for the business to become profitable as soon as possible. An imposing Director's desk was installed in the sitting room and this soon became the nerve centre for a throbbing busy-ness that invaded the shabby old house. Gone was the placid atmosphere of sleepy summer holidays, every corner of the whole building seemed to be full of noise and activity.

There was no space for Susie here. No place to crawl away in the night when the flickering flames of childhood fears crept over her elusive dream of a 'happy- ever- after' marriage. She had had to give up her ballet school when they left London and now that her son had joined his sister at a co-educational boarding school a huge emptiness filled her days. She missed the children more than she expected and the chattering and squabbling that sometimes drove her mad was replaced by an oppressive silence. There seemed no option but to resort to her 'one thing' and start all over again.

It was much more difficult to establish a new school in a rural community. Susie's professional background posed a threat to those who had no desire for a Royal ballerina treading upon their territory and it was more with the energy of despair than enthusiasm that she started a small class in a local barn. Her pupils were not the hand picked, finely bred daughters of the upwardly mobile professional classes who had swelled the numbers of her city school. The bodies of farmers' children (used to horse riding and haymaking) were of stockier build. Few had ever seen a live ballet performance and all lacked the blasé attitude of those who were accustomed to the predictable Christmas showings of the 'Nutcracker' and school matinees of 'Sleeping Beauty' at grand urban theatres.

Susie struggled to mould untrained limbs into the required regulation shape demanded by an examination syllabus which got stricter and more pedantic every year. The magic of dance, so passionately advocated by its founder Margot Fonteyn, seemed to become squeezed into ever more restricted channels. Even when she became an examiner herself Susie would give more credit to an occasional flash of star quality than the exact placing of a toe on a particular section of the calf muscle. For this, and other lapses into what were considered 'emotional responses', she was reprimanded by the Examiner of examiners.

She only became an examiner to escape from the growing tension of a marriage that had silted up like the mud in the millpond outside their bedroom window. Husband and wife had little respite from only each other's company except in the school holidays.

When the children came home family meals erupted into fierce debates between the new generation and the old. The changing views and growing teenage opinions challenged the traditions of their parents. Susie found herself caught up in arguments about issues she had never bothered to consider before and began to form new opinions of her own. The loft throbbed with loud music competing with the rhythm of the churning millstone in the adjacent building and the place felt like a family home again. Father, mother, daughter and son briefly reunited in a joyful holiday spirit at beach picnics, sailing outings and midnight swims but when the parents found themselves alone again, a grey mist of loneliness swirled between them.

They both retreated into their work, each building a wall around the separate empires they sought to construct. The only time they really talked was every evening at drinks' time in what Susie called their 'stress bubbles'. They would then vie with each other, as to who had had the busiest day through the smoke screen of their cigarettes preventing their eyes from making contact.

Susie's school gradually grew into a 'Kingdom of Dance' and from the safe isolation of the ivory tower, into which she was accused of retreating, she conducted numerous classes, re-arranged old ballets and composed new ones for over two hundred pupils and students.

She formed a youth ballet company in 1980. It was based on her own professional experience. Not for them a show of unconnected numbers, she told her pupils, they would give proper performances of real ballets, like 'Coppelia', Sleeping Beauty', Swan Lake' and 'Giselle'. Susie unfolded the knowledge she had packed away with her 'point' shoes and found it was as fresh as butterflies' wings.

The Isle of Wight Ballet Company did indeed bring alive a magic, infusing the young dancers with a vibrant energy reaching out to touch deeply the hearts of their enthusiastic audiences. Everyone on and off the stage was transported into a realm of enchantment where technical difficulties were forgotten and youthful bodies radiated with the light of their own unique grace.

The secret conveyed in 'The Little Prince', the first original work choreographed by Susie herself, seemed to epitomise the whole ambitious venture. 'What is essential is invisible to the eye, it is only the heart that sees rightly'.

Her husband introduced her to this poignant children's story and for a short time they became closer through their mutual love of the works of Antoine de Saint Exupery. Susie wrote of the profound impression made on her, when she was transforming 'The Little Prince' into the medium of dance, in her diary of summer 1980, 'I felt a power motivating me far beyond my own capabilities. It drove me relentlessly as if I was a mere vehicle for its vast force. The joy was overwhelming, like being in love.'

Choreography opened the dancing teacher's eyes and ears anew. As she listened intently to Elgar's 'Wand of Youth' suite, (the music chosen for the ballet), steps and patterns flowed out before her deepening insight. Sound and movement wove together creating a whole image with breath taking speed and clarity. All Susie had to do was to gather up and record what she saw in her mind as fast as she could. The excitement that motivated her spilled over into her pupils and they eagerly transformed the fleeting effervescence of their teacher's hurriedly scribbled notes into a captivating portrayal of enchantment.

Two outdoor performances of 'The Little Prince' were presented by The Isle of Wight Ballet Company on the green grass stage of a beautiful country mansion. Everyone was inspired. Dancers, audience, children, adults, women and men alike were caught up in the spirit of the strange and wonderful parable as it revealed its hidden secret through dance, the language of the soul.

Susie at last understood that dancing is an inner movement that no amount of training or technique can create. It moved like love through the still, sitting spectators, it spoke like truth upon the silent sun-drenched lawn, it shone like moonbeams in steps that were lighter than light and it sang like the 'laughter in the stars' that the Little Prince promised us we would hear. It was a true communion of all that is visible and invisible to the eye.

* * *

The woman is moved. She lays down the book of 'The Little Prince' upon the windowsill of the sunny box. She sighs. The nights are drawing in now.

It will be dark by the end of the afternoon. She feels the laughter that is so near to tears well up inside her.

'All the stars will be wells pouring out water for me to drink' the odd little voice had said, startling the crashed pilot in the desert, in Saint-Exupery's story. Her husband was also a pilot and took the part of the narrator in the ballet his wife created. It had been a magical time and when he presented Susie with a red rose at the end of the performance the romance of their engagement was briefly recaptured.

The woman draws deeply upon the well of her experience, each bucketful of memories she pulls up are surprisingly fresh. The Little Prince had had a rose of whom he was very fond. He felt so responsible for her that he put her in a glass cage. Wondering how the rose could breathe, the woman takes a deep breath. She is refreshed to drink in the remembrance that has matured and clarified like the best wine; sometimes still, sometimes sparkling like the stars in the cold black night.

The sky is darkening. A hush falls over the bare brown fields as rich as chocolate.

Birds seek a place to sleep in the red berry-laden mountain ash. The light dims. The interval is over. The woman comes in from the sunny box and takes her seat in front of the fire. The flames perform their mysterious dance and the curtain rises again.

* * *

Susie's next original ballet was called 'Voice of Light' inspired by Graham Sutherland's illustrations for Appollinaire's poems about Orpheus singing to the wild creatures. This innovative work opened the choreographer's world wider still. The realms of literature, art and music were a revelation to her and gave her courage to write her own scenario for the following production, 'The Miller's Damsel'. The story for the new work unfolded through the music of Bizet. She had never given her full attention to music before. She had always been too busy dancing. But now as she sat quite still hearing the intricacies of L'Arlesienne Suite the invisible black notes seemed to leap off the stave like dancing black ants and create their own form and meaning.

'Miller's Damsel' was the trade name of her husband's business. He was delighted when his wife dedicated her latest creation to the tenth anniversary of his milling and baking enterprise. This too was flourishing like The Isle of Wight Ballet Company. The ballet teacher and the businessman each enjoyed their own success and both became more ambitious. What they failed to attend to was the growing gulf between them.

Susie took on more and more until she descended from her ivory tower, perched precariously on the peak of her Kingdom of Dance, only on Sundays. By then she was in such a state of exhaustion that it blotted out all thought thus justifying a day of doing nothing. But the ageing dancer's body was beginning to protest. Agonising cramps, inflammation of the feet and stabbing pains plagued her in the night. She imagined these were self-inflicted wounds and tried to stifle her moans by stuffing a handkerchief in her mouth until morning came and she could have her first cigarette. The ground upon which she had built her Kingdom seemed to be disintegrating like dry rot in the very foundations of her life. It is said that if a kingdom is divided against itself, it will fall.

Susie fell twice. Once down a cattle grid, badly gashing her shin, and again at an examiner's course, rupturing her Achilles tendon. But she couldn't give up.

The panic stricken woman was too tightly wound up, like an alarm clock waiting to go off. No sooner was one production completed than the next temptation lured her on.

'Midsummer Night's Dream' was irresistible. Mendelssohn's famous musical overture demanded a huge mental and physical effort that surpassed all previous endeavours. Shakespeare's involved and ingenious plot gripped the mind of choreographer, relentlessly egging her on and on beyond the limits of her strength. But Susie continued to cling onto the 'lifeline of dance' to pull her struggling body up the crumbling walls of her tower.

Midsummer Night's Dream was the greatest success yet but it was only the adrenaline of panic and tension that generated sufficient energy for Susie to get through it.

The final work produced by the Isle of Wight Ballet Company was the same as the first. 'The Little Prince' had a life of its own. The well of Susie's creativity had run dry so she now relied upon the memory of her pupils and the magic of the story to revive this special ballet. It worked.

But in 1985 Susie's diary records, 'by now I have almost completely exhausted my energy. At the Annual Summer School I have to draw deeply on my diminishing reserves to teach the emotionally draining mad scene from 'Giselle'.

She goes on, 'after this I have a few weeks' rest before handing over the bulk of the teaching to my two assistants and assuming a less demanding role as overall consultant'.

But instead of improving with rest Susie's condition deteriorated disturbingly. The pain and exhaustion increased so that often she 'cannot walk without support, stand for more than a short time and eventually cannot even find the strength to lift the breakfast spoon to my mouth'.

A third and final fall down the steep, narrow staircase of the old mill house was caused by an acute vertigo attack. The forty-nine year old woman was hurled into a whirling black hole sucking her back through time to a place where a seven year old child lost her key.

* * *

The woman in the box cries out in distress, 'it's here, the key is in the door'.

But Susie cannot hear her calling. They are still divided, she and herself, both alone in time. A huge gulf separates them now but the long journey home is about to begin.

Chapter Five

THE JOURNEY BEGINS

By the beginning of 1986 her condition was looking serious. A doctor who specialised in medicine for performing artists heard of the former ballerina's plight. He invited her to the London hospital, where he practised, to undergo a series of intensive tests in an attempt to diagnose the cause of her alarming decline. Immediately an overwhelming sense of relief flooded her tense body. At last someone was taking control of her life. What was left of it. She sank, with remarkable ease, into what she guesses would be her final role. She found that she had no fear of death. It would solve everything. She imagined fading away gracefully in a fetching pink bed jacket murmuring 'Bless you my darlings,' to all those who would say 'Wasn't she marvellous' after she had gone.

This wonderful sense of well being continued to bring a growing peace of mind that was quite new to her. She wrote in her diary, 'Soon all stress and tension vanished as I had no energy left to worry. Whenever I became irritable, intolerant, jealous or self-pitying the physical effect was immediate and disastrous. I soon learned to stop these destructive feelings before they even started.'

Her prayer for 'somebody up there to switch me off' had been answered in a way she could not dispute. She felt everything had been taken out of her hands and the child-like faith, which she thought she had lost, came back to restore her soul in exactly the way the psalmist describes.

The diary continued, 'At last my spirit has been released from the dancer's body in which it has been imprisoned for so long. Like a freed bird it soars high and wide marvelling in ecstatic joy at the stunning beauty of creation. I become aware of the tremendous privilege of being a part of the miracle of Life and feel honoured to take my humble place among the trees, plants and birds which greet me through the open window each morning.'

One particular tree was to become of special significance in the following months. The ancient walnut tree clung precariously to the side of the millpond. The pond had been re-constructed too close to the tree's roots, when the old water wheel was replaced by a modern turbine engine at the beginning of the last century. Its hold on life seemed as tentative as that of the frail woman who spent many hours lying in bed gazing at its hollow trunk and broken branches. It seemed incredible that the tiny pink leaves of spring could be hidden in invisible buds that took longer and longer to appear each year.

Susie was given a phial of walnut oil by the osteopath's wife, a specialist in Bach flower remedies. She explained that the essence of this particular tree could help to give strength at times of great and traumatic change. Saint-Exupery described a tree 'that had taken its root within a derelict house and thence set forth on its quest for light.' He said 'the tale of its long struggle was written in the twisted trunk telling of the painful effort to break from the womb of darkness.' This made perfect sense to Susie as she felt something of the sort was happening to her body. The tree's quest ended when ' it rose majestic and serene, spreading forth its leafage like a banquet table for the sun's regalement suckled by the very heavens and gloriously nourished by the gods.'

Susie pondered long on the image of the old tree during that cold and lifeless February. The seed of a healing tree was planted in her imagination but she could not know then that when it germinated it would provide her with the structure upon which to rebuild her life. The Rainbow Tree had yet to unfold the colours of transformation.

Susie sank into a contemplative state that removed her mind from the distractions of the world around her. She sometimes felt it was easier to communicate with trees and dogs than with human beings.

The diary went on, 'All we need to believe is that Life is God and God is Life within us, around us, everywhere and always. All we need to do is just be. By loving Life with a poignant urgency I am no longer able to take anything for granted. I vow never again to be at the mercy of my body and the time has come to let it rest. I totally accept the physical pain and limitations as each day my spirit becomes stronger and healthier. I have bartered my body for the sake of my soul, which now needs to be nourished unhampered by the demands of a dancer's life. All I ask is to be allowed to remain a little longer on this peaceful plateau. I am not ready to climb again and know that my strength can only come from within.

A temporary boost, generated by drugs would damage the natural process of my body. Only a spiritual energy will equip me for the journey for which I am preparing'.

Journey! 'What journey?' Susie wondered.

* * *

It began with the remarkable week in a London hospital. She underwent daily tests, ex-rays, brain and lumber scans, all of which failed to bring any light on Susie's mysterious physical and mental state, but she existed more and more on what she called 'Cloud Nine'. She found she could reach this place, which was somehow above the severe and constant pain that inflamed her spine, by listening to music. Susie had never listened to music with such intense concentration before. There was nothing between her and the music. There was no story to unfold or transform into dance. She could relax without thought and just allow certain chosen pieces to pour into her whole body through a newly acquired head-set. The music flooded every fibre of her being until she was not aware of anything else, not even the pain.

When all the tests were completed, the doctor advised his patient to rest awhile, at the house of old friends, before returning home to the

Isle of Wight. Lying in bed on Sunday February 6, 1986 she recorded the moment that changed the entire course of her life.

'The familiar and much loved Shubert Noturno swept over, through and into me until I became one with the divine music and soared up to Cloud Nine.

Then I went on. On and beyond to terrifying lonely exposed heights that I have never experienced before. The light is blinding, as St. Paul said, the strength of the force, which is quite literally consuming me, is awe-full. It engulfs me with a power against which I am helpless. The love of God is burning me up. I am afraid it will become too strong and bright for my body to bear. I am afraid I will explode. We are all vehicles for God's love. Those who die without being aware of it are not able to bear the blinding burning power of its immensity but it comes through them to other people even when it is not in the dying themselves. Oh! It is getting clearer and clearer as I become more and more luminous. My soul keeps leaving my body. I cannot keep it captive any more.'

Susie must have cried out, for just then her friend came running in from the bathroom next door clutching a tin of 'Vim' in pink rubber clad hand. This comforting sight brought Susie back to earth with a bump.

'E. caught the string of my balloon just in time to prevent it floating away forever,' the diary concluded.

She was now in reckless mood! The 'geriatric ballerina' had a crazy desire to attend an impromptu Gala being presented to save Sadler's Wells Theatre from closure. This just happened to coincide with her release from hospital. Her saintly hosts agreed to accompany their friend who seemed to have gone beyond the bounds of reasonableness. All were caught up in the atmosphere of hopeful enthusiasm as soon as they arrived at the Royal Opera House.

Susie wrote, 'I felt weak and shaky but was so happy and thrilled to meet old ballet friends that I soared up to 'Cloud Nine' again without effort. I even bumped into Madam in the loo who greeted me effusively as one of her former protégés, then stood back to take a good look and exclaimed, 'Who are you?' before we both burst into laughter!'

When Susie had been safely escorted and gently settled into a comfortable seat in the centre of the orchestra stalls a small miracle occurred. Sitting directly in front of her seat was the doctor who had taken such excellent care of her during the previous week. It was a good thing he understood the impulsive nature of performing artists so well! He did not reprimand the patient who was supposed to be in bed, but joined in the general air of intense excitement.

The performance started with a delightfully spirited display from the Junior Royal Ballet School pupils. It brought back vivid memories of teaching young dancers who had now become esteemed members of to-day's ballet elite. They were all here that memorable night.

Later, Susie wrote, 'I was so enjoying myself when suddenly there was a violent explosion in my head. I was thrown into the familiar and dreaded dark void that spun me round without mercy. My hand shot out to clutch the seat in front of me, the doctor's hand held mine while my friend grasped the other one to try to steady my rocking body. As soon there was a suitable break I was led out to the foyer. By now I was shaking and vibrating without control. My head was spinning, my hands felt as if they had been electrocuted but my doctor took command of the situation with practised ease. All we needed, apparently, was a paper bag!'

The Opera House barman could not assist with this unusual request and just enquired whether Madam would like ice and lemon in her glass of water.

Susie managed to rally to the bizarre state of affairs with something of her renowned trouper's spirit. She suggested an S.T. bag from the ladies' cloakroom might do. It was just what was required to provide a makeshift oxygen mask to stop the hyper-ventilating attack from which she was suffering. Soon the immediate crisis was over.

With a little string pulling, reminding the theatre staff that she used to work in this place as well, Susie was allowed to lie down in some discomfort upon a small, hard chaise-long in the King's smoking room. Coats were piled on top of her, in the absence of any more appropriate covering, to try to restore the circulation of the shivering woman. Her main concern now was that her friends and doctor should not miss the rest of the gala. Eventually they were persuaded to leave Susie in the care of a St John's Ambulance nurse hastily summoned from the front of house. She told her patient she had waited three years to get this posting as she was a great opera and ballet fan. Susie assured the nurse that she would be quite alright on her own and encouraged her to return to the auditorium as well.

She lay back in solitary peace and closed her eyes.

Then the music from the distant stage floated seductively under the door. The strains of the famous Rose Adagio from 'Sleeping Beauty' reached the ears of the former princess. She rose from her bed just as if she had been awoken from a hundred years of sleep. She followed the hypnotic melody until she reached the door to the theatre. It seemed to open by itself but the scene it revealed was not the magical one of a fairy tale where wishes come true and spells are broken by the kiss of love.

This was no fantasy. The stage was empty except for one elderly woman. Dame Ninette de Valois was giving a stirring speech about Sadlers Wells Theatre, the foundation of the whole of the Royal Ballet. The passion, determination and conviction of her former boss convinced Susie that these were the qualities she needed now to give her the strength to live her life for real.

Chapter Six

THE LIGHT SHINES IN THE DARKNESS

Susie returned to the Isle of Wight with nothing to show for what had happened to her. She had been basking in the centre of attention before she left, the focus of concern and speculation as to what dramatic disease the specialists would diagnose. That they could not find anything wrong with her indicated to some that it was indeed nothing more serious than an acute menopausal crisis. They assured Susie that she would soon be her old self again. This was certainly what her husband wanted. He could not understand that there was no longer an old self to come back to. All the carefully crafted selves had been shattered, like so many distorted mirrors, leaving no image of their reflections behind. It was he, who everyone said was 'marvellous,' not Susie.

He assumed the role of carer for the wife who had no role left to clothe her nakedness. He shopped, he cooked, he brought her meals in bed. She longed to share what was happening to her but couldn't find the words to make him understand.

Her life had changed. His had not.

She could not turn back. He could not come with her.

It was her problem, not his.

She had to go on alone.

She had said 'Yes' to Life, though what that might be she had yet to learn.

During the next eighteen months Susie often felt as if she were on an intensive teaching course. Everything she was learning threw a new light upon her life. She described being, 'strapped to the bed with the big spotlight in the sky shining relentlessly into every dark corner'.

There was nowhere to hide now, no ivory tower into which to escape. She was often more helpless than wee Susie had been, confined to the top floor of the tall Edinburgh house, all those years ago. Her spine had become blocked top and bottom, so her osteopath informed her, restricting the spinal fluid like the flow of water in a blocked pipe. This was the cause of the disruption to the nervous system, the severe muscular weakness and the continual pain invading every fibre of the body. Susie told her osteopath that she did not need a body any more and it was her soul that mattered now. He was a wise and serious Frenchman who did not laugh at this strange remark. He gently suggested, 'It is useful to have something to carry the soul about in.'

But when Susie's body was asleep her soul took flight. She was on a voyage of discovery piercing dark, distant depths with a new light of understanding. She felt she had become a vehicle for the vast transforming force that used to motivate her choreographic efforts. Now she herself was being transformed.

'You will not find peace if you transform nothing according to the light that is yours; if you do not make of yourself a vehicle, a pathway, a portage.'

So said Antoine de Saint-Exupery, in his profound philosophy, 'The Wisdom of the Sands.' This amazing book, published after the author's mysterious death in 1944, greatly influenced Susie's thinking at that time. The constant references to 'the vehicle,' 'the light' and 'the house' resonated with her childhood images and now were taking on a new reality.

The words, 'I constrain you to build a house within yourself: once it is built there comes the visitant, who sets your heart aflame,' reminded her of God's house with all the little lights of children shining through its windows. Was she to become a house herself? She wondered, the Bible talks about being a temple for the Holy Spirit; perhaps this was what it meant? The hunger to learn the meaning of this 'Life' that held her to itself as surely as a tree holds a spring leaf drove her to question many well known passages with a bold curiosity.

These two books, the Bible and 'The Wisdom of the Sands', plus a small brown dog, were her constant companions as she lay in bed day after day. She thought deeply about everything she read and the meaning within the words touched hidden recesses in her aching body and nourished her starving soul. All she had left were feeling and thought.

Pain purified both from emotional distortion. She was not depressed, anxious or frustrated. There was no room for anything but her pain. She surrendered to it with the helplessness of a new-born babe. It freed her mind from the constrictions of the bodily activity that had dominated it for so long. She felt she was on rewind. She was going back to her beginning place to start all over again.

Her faith in Life grew. It lived in her like electricity lives in a flex, or a flame shines from a candle or sap flows through a tree. It chose to live in her. It must still have a purpose for her, but what value could she possibly be to Life in her current state of helplessness?

In February 1987, exactly a year after the blinding flash of enlightenment, which had concluded the week of tests in hospital, Susie wrote in her journal,

'Life, who is God, saw the vessel he had made for himself; cracked, spoilt, tarnished, damaged; filled with years of abuse. He alone saw that it could still be beautiful, still be useful. He took the vessel that is me and set to work to mend, to scour, to polish and restore his creation into something fitting for the spirit of Life to enter. While this painful process was taking place I was always aware of God's purpose being worked out through me. I did not understand what that was but I thankfully accepted the pain of re-creation in great humility, knowing that the tireless patience and care that God was bestowing upon me was a tremendous privilege'.

The discipline of a dancer's training stood her in good stead. When she had been privately coached for 'Giselle', in intimidating one to one sessions, by Dame Ninette de Valois, there was no need for her to be

45

told for what role she was being prepared. She did not question the judgement of her director then nor did she now. She put her whole trust in God who seemed to be in charge of her life. Her new vocation was to commit herself to whatever task He was training her for.

In order to progress along the spiritual path ahead of her, she sought a particular method or school of thought that would guide her on the daunting journey to find the Truth which is the quest of all religions. She considered Buddhism, from which she learned far more about the art of prayer and meditation than any church had ever taught her, but as a long suffering vicar advised, she eventually chose the Christian path. It was, he said, more readily available on the Isle of Wight than any of the Eastern philosophies that shed such fascinating new light on the mysterious being of Christ. It was a revelation to discover that the radical Jew who said 'God is spirit and they that worship Him must worship in Spirit and Truth' was not confined to the Christian religion.

Later on in her journey she found He was within and outwith all the great spiritual disciplines that mankind has followed throughout the ages.

The retired Anglican vicar, out of whose church she had angrily stomped when she still had ballet dancer's legs to stomp with, gently suggested that a 'rule', such as that followed by the monastic traditions, might be helpful. Reading morning and evening prayers could provide a structure to her day and act as spiritual exercises to strengthen and balance her passionate, but uncontrolled, new vocation. This made perfect sense to one who used to start every day at the barre preparing her muscles for the tasks they were required to perform later.

The Book of Common Prayer stated that at least two people should be gathered together to perform these simple acts of daily worship. In the absence of another willing human being, the small brown dog was happy to oblige. Each morning and evening he took his place in his favourite 'pew', on the softest corner of the duvet, with the eagerness of a new convert. He especially enjoyed sung Evensong on the radio joining the cathedral choirs with a rare reverence and musicality unusual to find in a dog. But then, Trumpet was an extremely unusual member of the canine species. It was thought that he had a Besenji ancestor from whom he had inherited his yodelling and versatile voice and extraordinary skill at shadow dancing. He seldom left his mistress's side. On the days when she managed to cross the challenging gulf between the bed and the chair, upon which her clothes were draped, Trumpet would sit silently waiting while she laboriously clad her painful limbs with sweater and slacks. He did not leap up and down or bark impatiently, like most dogs, but quietly accompanied the woman as she slowly walked out into the garden with the aid of a hazel walking stick. Whenever she stopped to rest he would amuse himself with a particularly interesting smell or dig a small hole as if this were exactly the place he would have chosen to stop himself.

Sometimes they got as far as a little copse, between two ploughed fields, a short distance from the busy mill house and bakery of her husband's thriving business.

It became their very own cathedral. Choirs of birds and lofty windows, stained with many colours from the foliage of self planted trees, created a sacred atmosphere. There the woman and the small, brown dog worshipped their creator in the spirit of the sweet air they breathed which truly seemed to be 'the compassionate breath of God', as Christ is described in Sufism. They were at peace in this simply beautiful oasis, left undisturbed by generations of farmers who cultivated the land all around it. The little copse had grown naturally into its own shape, season after season, year after year, according to the ways of the wind, the sun and the rain. Untouched by human hands there was a natural beauty about the place. On the days when she was confined to bed she imaged she could recreate its presence in her mind. She seemed to be losing her sense of time and space. Sometimes she felt she could travel through both without moving her body at all. Just to remember was to make the experience of being there as real as breathing.

Susie's writing took on a poetic character with all the licence she used to incorporate in the stories she invented for her ballets. The process of committing the written word to paper soothed and steadied her wandering thoughts and gave her a way of understanding what was happening to her. The love she felt flowing through all the pain seemed to reside in the core of all living things.

This poem was written on one of those days when she was unable to rise from the bed.

'From afar I hail the little copse,
The distance to the eye does not defy my undaunted soul,
With one ecstatic leap she soars through time and space
To the heart of that beloved place
Which is my sanctuary of peace.

Still held in tender bark,
Enfolding bough, cradles now, my spine in sweet embrace.
The trees are nearer, clearer here in the eye of my heart
I am apart of the shape of you
Though parted from your touch.

The breeze in the leaves of the trees
Makes shadows shimmer and sunlight glimmer through dappled holes
Shielding me from the blinding light that pierced my soul
With the unbearable pain of love,
The love that is born through pain.

The silent cloak of love
Devours the pain, holds again my aching head upon the bed
Of soft remembered moss, which soothes and cools,
Until love and pain are one,
Conflicts cease, and all is peace.'

Writing became a lifeline to the solitary woman. It created a safe place into which she could retreat from the increasing despair that filled the gulf between her husband and herself. The harder she tried to communicate her fears about the future of their relationship the less he seemed to hear her. He said she was emotionally unbalanced, it was part of her condition and everything would be all right when she regained her senses. But he missed the whole point. She was in her right senses for the first time since the beginning of their marriage. She couldn't pretend any more. Although she was grateful for his caring and concern for her physical and material needs there was no escape from the reality of the spiritual and emotional distance that separated them..

The situation became intolerable. She had to get away, but where could she go and how? She couldn't drive any more and she knew of nowhere in the vicinity which might be able to offer any help.

A Catholic friend came to her rescue. She knew some old nuns who were struggling to keep a large Victorian Priory going with the help of some devoted members of the 'laity'. They would take anyone, the good Catholic told the Anglican, who was so lapsed that she had almost forgotten her baptism in the Church of Scotland.

The nuns agreed to allow her to make a weekly retreat staying overnight in the comfortingly shabby guest room with gas fire and hand knitted hot water bottle cover. The regularity and peace of these visits soothed and steadied her. She found great solace in joining the nuns' daily prayers and the chanting of the psalms calmed her inner turmoil. She started taking communion again. It felt as if a compassionate family had taken her in from a storm and it was natural to share their spiritual, as well as their earthly food. It therefore came as a great shock when she was told that it was against the rules for non-Catholics to take Communion and she could not be allowed to continue this unlawful practise. She said she was sure that Jesus wouldn't have excluded her but then, He didn't make the rules of the Church.

The only solution was to join the club even although the trappings and traditions of the Christian religion seemed far removed from the simplicity of the humble Nazarene carpenter who called people out of the synagogues and onto the hillside and seashore to hear him preach. She needed desperately to belong to something and to have an anchor to stay the drifting currents that threatened to sweep the remnants of her life away.

She became a Catholic. She was even given a new name, 'Julianna', after Julian of Norwich, who had received several divine revelations during a mysterious illness. However, it didn't stick any more than the label, 'Roman Catholic' and she resumed the childhood diminutive of her baptismal name, 'Susie'.

* * *

The woman has as much difficulty now, with the establishments of religion, as she did then. She has retained her simple belief that God is Life and Life is God and that the energy of Life is Love. Wasn't that what the Man said? Love God and love each other and everything else falls into place.

She knows it is only her faith that has brought her home. The journey from the Isle of Wight to Scotland has taken ten years and a most unusual route via India, the East end of London, Russia and the Lake District. But it now seems clear that this is the place that was waiting for her all along.

The re-wind of her life has stopped whirring. Life lies before her, like an empty cassette, absorbing the chill autumn silence of the dying light.

The sunny box is getting cold.

Chapter Seven

TIME TO GO HOME

The woman sits spinning. The afternoon sunshine brings welcome warmth to the sunny box. The frail fibres flowing through her hands are like the threads of time. She is spinning a web out of herself with the faith of the spider. The spider is precariously suspended in space hanging between the upper corner of the open porch door and the frame on the opposite side. What tenacity this tiny creature displays, not knowing if she will reach her unseen destination. She holds on to the substance of herself with inspiring perseverance quite literally spinning her own life-line. This is what the woman is doing for herself.

* * *

By 1987, a year and a half after her dramatic experience in the London hospital, Susie was beginning to regain her strength. The first thing she did, when she was fit enough to travel, was to go home to Scotland. Her mother had recently been forced to give up the Edinburgh house where the youngest of her four children had been born in 1935. The daughter was 52 now and her mother was 87.

It had been a tremendous wrench for her mother to pack up her life into a few boxes and suitcases. She was no longer Mrs. Alexander of Garscube Terrace, known by a wide circle of affectionate friends and respectful tradesmen. She was just one old lady, in a home in Creiff, with numerous others who had also lost their identities.

Her daughter had had a similar experience.

Susie had eventually vacated the mill house and taken up a reclusive residence in a small outbuilding in the orchard. The original intention was to use this as a spinning shed but as the relationship between husband and wife deteriorated, the need to create a space for herself became imperative.

The spinning wheel had come into her life quite unexpectedly. Soon after the convalescing woman took up knitting, when her hands were strong enough to hold the needles, a neighbour told her of a spinning wheel for sale in the next village. It would be good for her to have an interest, the well-meaning person said, but neither she nor Susie could have foreseen how much this new skill would give her. The gentle rhythm of the turning wheel restored a sense of equilibrium and co-ordination in her weak and shaky body, but more than that, it calmed her agitated mind with a steady flow of thoughtless concentration. The spinner called her wheel Sophia, not realising at the time that this was name for the Goddess of Wisdom. No other could have been more apt for the ancient craft which taught her more than any books or words.

* * *

The woman breathes a sigh of relief. The threads of time are beginning to connect now. It is as if both the past and the future are presently held in her hands. She feels that she can hold herself like the mother she so wanted to be and comfort the child within her. Is it possible, she wonders, to go back and repair the tapestry of her life and to fill in the missing bare patches? Could they be woven into the fabric of the future and strengthen the place where she sits in between what was and what will be? As the story unfolds, like the spider's web from within herself, the spinner has an image of the web radiating out into unknown corners of a world beyond her vision. It is not a trap but a way out that connects her inner self to rest of life.

* * *

Susie was seeking a way out of her life when she first went home to Scotland. The relationship with her mother took on a new understanding and brought both women solace and comfort during the difficult changes they were under going. Susie's pace had slowed down to match that of her elderly mother and they were like two old ladies together now. They had time to spare for each other and talked deeply for hours about the renewed faith they had both found in the enforced simplicity of their reduced circumstances. They rejoiced in the glory of Perthshire and subsequently, when Susie started driving again, revelled in exploring the surrounding countryside. They would hire a car and tour around this spectacular part of Scotland, stopping for picnics and ice creams like children out on a half term treat. They both fell in love with their native land, exhilarated by the beauty of heather bordered lochs, the majesty of sweeping hills and the crystal clear freshness of the air. They often felt as if Susie's father graced them with his generosity of spirit and shared their newfound joy.

As these visits became longer and more frequent, the daughter found a cottage to rent near her mother's home in Crieff. She felt so much better in the Northern air and flourished like a plant transferred back to its natural environment. Perhaps the solution to the problem of her current feeling of homelessness would be to return to her roots and buy a small property in Scotland. She had recently inherited a modest legacy from a maiden aunt and imagined purchasing something traditional with a lovely view where she could live with Sophia, the spinning wheel and Trumpet, the little brown dog. The attractive idea grew in her mind and she set her heart upon finding the cottage of her dreams.

God had something completely different in mind.

India was not a country that held any interest for Susie until her daughter made an adventurous trip to the sub continent after leaving school and before going to university. She had been greatly impressed by the philosophy and insight of an Indian gentleman who ran a creativity centre for deprived children in Gujerat. Mr Purwar was now in London on a lecture and workshop tour and the young woman wanted to bring him home to the Isle of Wight for the weekend and introduce him to her parents. When the dark brown man in snowy white Ghandi-style cotton met Susie he bowed politely placing his palms together in the customary 'Nemaste' of Hindu greeting.

'You are most welcome to visit my very small house with no bedroom and Indian style toilet your daughter will explain' he said all in one breath. The frail woman smiled politely back, thinking to herself, 'no way.'

But, having failed to find a cottage for sale near her mother, her need to get away from the small square shed in which she had confined herself became more and more urgent and Mr Purwar's invitation seemed to offer the only way out.

To go to India was a crazy thing to do at her age and especially considering her precarious state of body and mind. She had never travelled abroad on her own and had little idea of the practicalities that such a trip would entail. On her next trip to India Susie's gallant daughter agreed to escort her mother as far as Delhi, but after that, 'You're on your own, Mum,' she said.

Most people thought she was mad but the Catholic nuns at the Priory said it was God's will. As an incredible stroke of serendipity they had founded a Benedictine convent near Bangalore and were only too pleased to dispatch the new convert off on a visit to their Indian sisters. Susie was plied with a variety of gifts to take with her, ranging from hand crocheted Bible covers and sacred heart bookmarks to paper clips and home made jam.

A Catholic friend gave her a finger rosary to help her on her journey, and although she had not yet learnt how to use it, the little silver ring proved to be a Godsend that gave her courage and strength in her weakest hour.

On October 4, 1988, on the wings of many prayers, mother and daughter set off from London airport. Susie still intended to move to Scotland as soon as she returned and had left packed suitcases, the spinning wheel and the dog basket all ready on the Isle of Wight, waiting to be collected after the trip. She would just have to stay in the rented cottage until God provided her with something else. She thought she had made the final break from a dying marriage but it wasn't quite as easy as she imagined. She was to learn many things in India that would help her to move on in an entirely different way to any she had known before.

Chapter Eight

AN INDIAN EXPERIENCE

Susie was like a starved woman confronted with a feast when she arrived in India. She had not realised how hungry she was for spiritual food until she stepped out of the plane into a world she did not even know existed. The extravagance of vocabulary, which tumbled out of her Indian journal, did not exaggerate the wealth of colour, sound, taste and movement that invited her to join the great Festival of Life all around her.

The words have lost none of their vibrant energy while lying dormant in a forgotten file these past 13 years. The woman relaxes. She had nothing to do but to listen to Susie's account of that amazing time.

'I seem to float effortlessly on a wave of excitement from Heathrow Airport to the capital city of India on Tuesday, October 4th. After a hilarious bus journey from the airport, bumping and lurching at top speed past a few laconic white cows, and slumbering, shrouded figures on the roadside (not always recognisably human), we finally reach the centre of Delhi. The shabby, romantic pillars of the Connaught Square loom eerily out of the dusk like some forgotten film set. We take a taxi to the apartment where we are staying with a friend of my daughter arriving at four o'clock in the morning.

We spend the next five days exploring the city. My daughter, the experienced traveller, delights in showing her astonished mother the sights; the shops, the snake charmers, the street musicians, the fabulous markets and the best cafes, where we revive ourselves with chapattis and mango ice cream.

Each morning we set off in one of the numerous rickshaws that manoeuvre with hair-raising speed and breathtaking skill through the chaotic traffic. Ancient cars, over flowing buses, precariously and variously loaded bicycles dodge between wandering cows and sleeping dogs with much honking, shouting and gesticulating. It's all part of the fun.

Never have I experienced such a rich feast for all the senses. Wool, cotton and silk of every colour and texture, fruit, nuts and flowers of infinite variety are artistically displayed on numerous tiny stalls. Bright elegant clothes worn with style and flair and fresh garlands in shiny black hair dance to the music of calling vendors, piping beggars and singing children.

The whole of life is celebrated in the spirit of Carnival. Amidst the crowd, pools of beseeching eyes and gleaming white smiles light up dark faces and send my hand again and again into my purse. Ingenuity and imagination are displayed in all the tiny stalls, even the humblest and most mundane of wares are presented with pride and care. The resourcefulness, patience and cheerful perseverance of the shop-keepers are hard to resist. Beautiful hand dyed scarves, cashmere shawls, embroidered pyjamas, bangles, beads and earrings made of shells and feathers are like jewels opening up before me. I come home laden with treasures of far more than material value. I am full of admiration for the vitality of these remarkable people who have so little of what we have and so much of what we have not.

My daughter leaves for Calcutta on Saturday, so our hostess and her angelic daughter, who have received us so graciously into their simple home, take me to the Brahma Kumari Centre for meditation. The noise, dirt and aggression of the busy street cease to exist the instant we step inside the cool, tranquil hall. We sink silently into our lotus positions on the marble floor beside other motionless figures.

Not a glance or a word is needed to tell me what to do and all thoughts fall away leaving my mind free to receive the spirit of Truth, whatever name we may call it. The same indefinable quality resides in all our hearts, whoever we are and wherever Life has placed us and as soon as we realise this, all differences are dissolved and we are at peace.

Next morning I am up before dawn to catch the plane to Bangalore. I am met by Rajan, sent by the Abbess of the Benedictine Abbey at Kothanur, 7 kilometres out of town. I had not known of the existence of the sister community of the nuns on the Isle of Wight until a few months ago but my smiling young escort reassures me that I will not be greeted as a stranger.

The short journey by scooter rickshaw takes us through the garden city and onto increasingly rough roads surrounded by fertile red soil with unrecognisable crops. When we reach Shanti Nyliam, meaning House of Peace, I see the Abbey is set in a farm jointly run by the Catholic nuns and the Hindu village people.

As I see a robed woman driving a small flock of sheep through a pillared vineyard and calling to them by name, it is as if scenes from the Bible are coming to life before my eyes. Another washes her feet in a huge stone stepped well, and more, with wide brimmed straw hats perched on top of their veils, work in the rice fields.

Tiny birds play on the giant sugar canes while a few cows amble past on their way to the open byre where they spend the nights. A small bakery with faggot oven, a large shed of laying hens, groves of coconuts and papaya trees, surrounding plots of vegetables and grain, complete the grounds of this self sufficient community. I am to be fed with heavenly food of both bodily and spiritual varieties during the next five days.

Each morning my heart and I rise with the sun from the hard, narrow little bed in my tiny cell-like room with en-suite closet. I am delighted with its simplicity undisturbed by anything unnecessary, like carpet, bedside lamp, mirror, shower or toilet paper. I have everything I need but no more. Nothing is taken for granted. Light, darkness, rain, sun, soil and water are all fully appreciated and valued even when they cause hardship. Frequent power cuts, floods and droughts are accepted as part of life like the seasons and, on my part, with a growing awareness of all Life's free gifts. I write a little prayer of gratitude.

'As the sun sets my heart goes back into you, giver of the day, to be held in the silence of your love which cloaks the sleeping earth. The heat descends into a soft darkness, the song of bee-eaters, green parrots and kingfishers fade into a quiet, still repose. I sit, kneel or lie upon the cool floor of the spacious, stone chapel and join in the gentle chants of evening prayers. Then, as I walk back to the guest house through the intoxicating fragrance of exotic blooms and the nocturnal sounds of croaking frogs and barking dogs, I know nothing will disturb my deep sleep of peace.'

Just before I left home I had received the address of my 'prayer-link', one of Mother Teresa's Missionaries of Charity. She had recently been moved from the rigours of working with the poor in the city of Trivandram to a remote coastal area on the Southern shores of India eight hundred miles from Bangalore.

It sounded idyllic and I had written to ask if I could pay her a visit. I received a welcoming letter back with instructions of how to reach her tiny village by plane and bus. None of my Indian friends had heard of Kothanur and it was nowhere to be found on the map so it was not without considerable trepidation that I set out into the unknown once again. I do not know whether I am invited for tea or a fortnight or whether anyone will meet me but the nuns at Shanti Nyliam say they will pray for me on my journey. I would have found a phone call or telegram more reassuring but such modern facilities are out of the question.

The flight on October the fourteenth is delayed four times and departs from Bangalore nearly five hours late but I am amazed to find that I feel nothing but a calm composure that all will be well. This prayer business seems to be working.

When I eventually arrive at Trivandram Airport I find no less than four people there to meet me. They are still smiling after the long wait. I am beginning to realise that time has a different dimension here. I spend the night with these kind cousins of somebody's sister's husband (I forget whose) and enjoy the first and last shower for over a week.

The two young men, who had been dispatched from Kothanur to escort me back there, are eager to set off early the following morning. The dusty, crowded bus is crammed with men, women and children hot and dripping *and smelling of sweat. We lurch precariously from bump to pothole for one and a half bone shaking hours. We drive past small hamlets nestling in rich, red terraced soil, scattering chickens, bicycles, excited children and women water carriers in our erratic path. On the roadside men and more women are breaking up stones under coconut leaf umbrellas and every now and again there is a busy crowd around one of the many village water pumps. Whole families wash everything they possess. Children, hair, teeth, clothes, cooking bowls, pots and pans are scrubbed and scoured with tremendous vigour.*

The excitement accelerates and the white smiles grow as we approach the village of Kothanur. My escorts point out three stout nuns walking towards us who greet us effusively as we climb down from the sticky bus. My link, Sister Mercy, is the plumpest and has the widest grin.

I follow the chattering group down a narrow, sandy track and suddenly a vast, pink beach with sparkling turquoise rollers breaking upon the distant shore fills my eyes and heart with wondrous awe. A small squat building surrounded by square white walls sits modestly beside a huge church which dwarfs its appealing simplicity. This is to be my home for the next eight days.

As there is no hotel for miles around, I am given the rare privilege of staying at the convent with the community of eight nuns. I feel honoured to share their frugal life amongst the poor fisher folk and tapioca farmers whom they tend. There are no guest facilities here so a bed is hastily erected in the entrance hall behind two old wardrobes acting as screens to give me a little privacy. I discover that this is the only room into which the public are permitted entry so I have to share it with many daytime visitors from the local community.

I am shown a squat loo across the yard with customary tap and jug in place of toilet paper and a stone trough behind a wall with bucket and cup for washing self and clothes. Then lunch arrives. I had rashly asked God to let me experience poverty so the fullness of his answer should not have come as a surprise. I tackle my solitary meal with gusto and gratitude although the dried fish pieces, boiled tapioca roots, (a bit like gluey potatoes), shredded coconut and a thermos of powdered milk are not exactly appetising.

I sleep in happy peace all afternoon despite the drenching heat, noisy fan and the impatient clattering, chattering crowd of villagers waiting to catch a glimpse of the strange creature who has descended into their midst. When I emerge, like a weird animal from its cage, I am greeted with inquisitive stares and noisy voices which follow me as I go about my ablutions and almost into the loo itself.

The parish priest comes to take me to five o'clock mass in a tiny church high up in the hills above the bay. The service is all in the local dialect of Malayam, but the meaning of the words transcends the barriers of language and I am immediately swept into the naked sacredness of this unscarred part of the world.

After church I am taken down to the seashore to meet the local fishermen. As the priest and I walk across the warm honey and pink sand to approach the roughly hewn log boats I see a scene as ancient as that of the Galilean Sea two thousand years ago. We sit down in an incomplete circle watching the magnificence of the setting sun. The waves become calm and a gentle dusk enfolds us in a communal silence. Someone draws on the sand and a quiet stillness spreads among us with an unspoken feeling of mutual awe. There is an unseen presence here that is acknowledged by us all and I know that the empty place in our circle has been filled completing our incompleteness in the unity of God's love. I feel closer, at this eternal moment, to these simple Indian fishermen than my own kith and kin.

I am awake next morning before the first church bell rings at five a.m. Carefully extracting the sleeping cockroach from my sandal, I grope my unsteady way across the still dark courtyard. A mouse and a giant spider are waiting to greet me but I am learning to live in peace with my fellow creatures and have a quick cold sluice from the water trough before hastily dressing in time for morning prayers.

I am amazed by the emptiness of the vast church. Its cathedral proportions seem incongruous in this tiny seaside village. No chairs or benches disturb the stark simplicity of the lofty building and the only decoration is a startling life sized crucifix bearing a black Christ hanging

61

above a rough granite altar. The whole spirit of the place is utterly different from anything I have encountered at home and yet it seems much more real.

After Mass I go with Sister Mercy to see the morning catch on the beach plunging straight into the tension of the fish auction. We, like the poor, select only the cheapest boniest varieties that are left after the merchants have had their pick. The attention I attract embarrasses me and the plucking fingers, at my skirt and heartstrings, make me wish I were black and anonymous.

We return to the convent for breakfast of chapatis, finger bananas, a scraping of honey and the inevitable thick sweet tea then I am briskly whisked off into the ambulance bus waiting to take the sisters to their weekly dispensary in a neighbouring hill village. This takes place on the church steps on which a trestle table is set up. Bottles of pink and white powder and boxes of pills of the same colour are arranged carefully upon it. Two buckets of boiling water are fetched in order to mix up the concoctions before they are dispensed among the long queue of waiting poor. My job is to tear up newspapers into small squares in which to wrap the pills and make stoppers for the assortment of, usually dirty, bottles into which the pink and white ' medicine' is poured. The value of the care with which it is administered far outweighs any other kind of benefit.

I have been forbidden to take photographs, as it is against the rules of the Missionaries of Charity, but I try to sketch my impressions on some spare scraps of newspaper. The depravation here seems much more extreme than that of the fishing community but the gratitude for so little is the same. I am heartened by the humanity of these people and find myself questioning the true meaning of poverty.

There is great excitement when a young white woman appears. I am eagerly bid to commune with another of my species. She is a peace worker from Florida. We both relish the opportunity to exchange experiences and relax into colloquial English for a while but soon I am called away as it is time to go home. After a long, hot trudge up the hill and a long hot wait,

62

we squeeze in a small packed bus that drops us off at the convent. I am filled to overflowing with all that I am learning and fall into a meditative snooze after lunch.

Too soon, I am abruptly awakened by Sister Mercy. She whisks me off to evensong in the local hospital, hardly giving me time to grab a scarf for my tousled head or push my swollen feet into my dusty sandals. I hasten to catch up with her impatient stride.

The monotonous, meaningless chanting of dutiful women does nothing to lift me out of my sluggish self. Then a young girl's voice soars above the others taking my soul up into the freedom of a flying bird and my spirits are lifted again. After the service I end up skipping round the church with a group of giggling children.

Getting up at five o'clock every morning is becoming a struggle and the strain on my fragile body is beginning to tell. A special breakfast, prepared for a visiting priest, and which I am allowed to share helps to revive me. He zooms in on an ancient bicycle booming a beaming 'Good morning' in a surprising Anglo-Indian-Irish accent. The unusual luxury of fried eggs, bread and butter, a whole pot of honey and a baked banana sets me up for the day's expedition to the tapioca plantation.

This is high up in the hills where we set up the trestle table in front of a community centre for pre-school children and post-school girls. The inevitable pink and white medicines are dispensed to an accompaniment of English nursery rhymes and the clacketty-clack of ancient typewriters. When our work is finished I am taken on a tour of the village consisting of a clutch of mud huts clustered round raised wooden paths. The view of the bay below takes my breath away and I imagine plunging into the cool sparkling sea but Sister Mercy's voice calling me back to the bus shatters my brief dream.

I play truant from Mass next morning. I may not be on holiday but my' 'link's' bossiness is beginning to irritate. I am scolded for not reciting the Rosary under my breath on the bus journeys as the nuns do, questioned about the regularity of my Bible study and forbidden to hang my knickers on the washing line on the convent roof. I can only suppose that, to those who do not wear any beneath their all-concealing saris, the sight of such Western decadence is shocking.

I savour the rare peace of a solitary stroll along the deserted beach. Then I am spotted by a fisherman, who introduces himself, in halting English, as Pius. He invites me to take tea and rice biscuits in his nearby hut. He and I are served like royalty by his little wife while two tiny children peep out nervously from behind her skirt. I am late for breakfast when I return to the convent, incurring further disapproval from Sr. Mercy.

I am ashamed of my growing intolerance at the continual hassle and noise from the first bell at 4.45a.m. until the last at 9p.m. The chanting women, the continual pop music blaring over the communal loud speaker system, the muttered Rosaries and even the nuns' raucous laughter during the evening hour of recreation grate on my ears and set my nerves on edge. I pray that I may acquire a little of the sisters' cheerful acceptance of their circumstances and hope that my irritation does not show. I think it must have done, for next day, on the way back from a visit to a weaving centre set up by the Government, Sr. Mercy suddenly stops the bus at a beautiful beach and commands me to take a swim. Wonderful, except I have nothing to wear. I make do with T. shirt and two pairs of knickers, carefully disguised with my scarf, and splash joyfully in the crystal clear water under the watchful eye of my 'Indian Nannie'. I feel a warm surge of affection for the smiling woman who has been landed with the embarrassment of her 'sick and suffering link' actually coming to stay. It would have been much easier for both of us just to pray for each other at a comfortable distance.

My prayer for privacy is also answered. God seems to anticipate my needs before I have even put them into words. On Sunday the nuns go out all day to the neighbouring villages to teach the children the rudiments of Catholicism by rote, a practise I thought went out with the Middle Ages. I find myself alone all day to reflect upon the strange, the difficult, the wonderful and above all, the humbling experience of sharing the life of these people who are so different from any others I have ever met. I vow to make *amends for my selfishness tomorrow and to try to find some way of thanking this impoverished community for their hospitality to a complete stranger.*

God answers my unspoken intention with His usual extravagance.

The jolly little Mother Superior invites me to accompany her to a Government farm where she plans to buy chickens to provide the residents of Kothanur with a ready supply of eggs and meat. She accepts with alacrity my offer to pay for them upping her order to an astounding eight dozen which just about cleans me out of my entire supply of rupees. Numerous protesting bundles of frenzied chicks, tied leg to leg, are thrown unmercifully into the back of the truck. Perhaps the little Mother realised that many of them would not survive the stifling homeward journey and had taken the opportunity to make up the numbers of those who would die.

All of a sudden it is my last evening and everyone wants their photograph taken after all. Unfortunately it is raining. This unexpected occurrence is cheerfully overcome and the entire village seems to crowd into the convent reception room/my bedroom. The choir, the priest, the giggling girls, Pius and his family and several other fisher folk take up pose after pose. Every flash of my camera is greeted with screams of delight and enthusiastic applause. We exchange farewell presents of home made cards and pictures, my clock, my only hankie and the scarf I wore for the memorable swim. We hug and hug again, moved beyond words as we keep smiling through our tears. After the final, final 'good-bye' I resign myself to the arduous journey back to Bangalore with a mixture of relief and sadness.

* * *

The guesthouse at Shanti Nyliam seems like a five star hotel and I surrender to the exhaustion I have been holding at bay for the last few days. Immediately a raging fever inflames my spine and I am confined to my hard little bed until the saintly Benedictine nuns move me into the main building so that they can nurse me more easily. Their quiet, unfussy care is a balm to my aching head after the hustling bustle of Kothanur, but my condition worsens and I cannot sleep. Even propped up on three mattresses, newly stuffed with cotton from this year's trees, my back still throbs with a bruising pain all night long.

I try to prepare myself for the forthcoming journey to Ahmedabad where I am to spend the final part of my trip staying with Mr. Purwar in his 'very small house' etc.

I stagger about the convent garden with the aid of the folding walking stick. I certainly feel extremely disabled and worried about my ability to travel alone all the way up to the North of this vast country. Of course, the nuns offer their customary prayers but their faith exceeds mine as I become weaker and weaker.

When the ninth day of November comes I have no choice but to put myself into God's hands and climb painfully into the rickshaw booked to take me to catch the early morning flight from Bangalore to Bombay.

I remember the finger Rosary and the words of the thoughtful friend as she gave it to me, 'Just put this on your finger and say the 'Our Father' and 'Hail Mary' prayers over and over again and you'll be all right.' I do as I was told and soon my anxious thoughts are absorbed in the soothing repetition of the prayers.

The rickshaw deposits me at the airport and I enter the small plane in a zombie-like state until it delivered me at Bombay. I sit on a hard, sticky, plastic chair for the next four hours waiting for the last lap of the journey. After a short local flight to Ahmedabad I slowly descend the steps from the small plane to the hot tarmac below and a slow smile of relief spreads across my tired face. Mr Purwar is waiting with a much bigger smile of welcome and a bouquet drooping of roses. The silver ring is still on my finger. As I quietly remove it and put it carefully in my pocket, I give thanks to God. I realise later that my mistake had been to pray that God would help me to cope instead of having the faith to know that I can always cope with His spirit inside me. It was only in my own extreme weakness that I understood His strength.

On arriving home, we had a delicious meal consisting of fresh *vegetables, lentils, dhal, chapattis and peanut chutney. My bed, in Mr. Purwar's very small house with no bedroom, is a mattress which he pulls down from a cupboard full of mattresses, and lays on the floor. As there is only one room, he sleeps neatly upon a shelf which is cunningly concealed behind a curtain. I am beginning to realise that this simple life-style has many advantages. Housework is minimal when there are no tables and chairs to dust, no carpet to Hoover or beds to make.*

The mattress is stowed away next morning and Mr. Purwar shows me a small space underneath his bed-shelf where I may put my belongings. Fortunately they are few. He then gives me a large orange cushion to sit on while I sip a cup of hot sweet tea. I am feeling much better and we are going sightseeing.

Mr. Purwar invites me to take a seat, side-saddle, behind him on his scooter and we set off, waving 'Good-bye' to his eighty eight year old mother who has suddenly appeared from nowhere. (I discover later that she sleeps underneath the kitchen table.) We stop off to collect the mail and park beside two tethered camels and a group of youths who seem to spend all day lounging cheerfully on an old iron bedstead outside the post office. They are still there when we return at dusk.

I am shown an extraordinary sand stone temple when we reach the centre of the city. Mr. Purwar says it was constructed over a thousand years ago. The intricate carvings, immaculately preserved in the dry heat of Gujerat, depict scenes from Hindu mythology. The characters weave a story that conveys its meaning in a timeless and visual language of dramatic effect.

Our next stop is at an ancient step well which I find even more impressive. It is like an upside down cathedral covering a vast area on the surface which conceals several hidden underground chambers leading down to the well itself. Each floor is embellished with carvings of even greater artistry than those of the temple.

The guide explains that many generations of stone- masons devoted, and often sacrificed their lives to the construction of this unique building. We descend the unprotected and precarious stairways moving further and further into the deep, dark heart of the well itself. Far above, an open skylight sheds an eerie sheen upon the green-black water.

This was the meeting place of women, the suicide place of the desperate, the whispering place of lovers, as well as the place where water was drawn for hundreds of years.

Depth, height; dark, light; shadow, tomb; sun, womb;
Walls, cave; pillars, space; builders, birds; women, words;
Love, breath; life, death; it is all here.

All Mr. Purwar's friends are poets, artists and musicians like himself and although materially poor are generous in spirit. Every meal is treated as a feast. A few cheap and simple ingredients are transformed with flair and artistry into an experience of creative celebration. We sit, cross-legged, on the floor around numerous colourful and tasty dishes dipping into them with chapattis held only in our right hands. Left hands are reserved for more basic functions and kept out of sight behind our backs. We converse in the universal language of the eyes, facial expressions, gestures, laughter and the shared enjoyment of our communal meal.

We receive each other openly, holding the moment between us in mutual gratitude for Life, which has brought us together in this particular place and time. All the differences of culture, creed, race and background dissolve and we become as brothers and sisters of one family. This is the communion I have been searching for. This is more meaningful than any ritual I have ever experienced in Church and I can't help feeling that this is what Jesus meant when he said, 'Do this in remembrance of me'. After all He wasn't in a church Himself at the time, but in an ordinary room in an ordinary house having an ordinary meal with friends.

The main purpose of my stay here is to visit the Sarjan Creative Education Centre, which Mr. Purwar set up in 1976, for orphaned and destitute children. After a severe flood, many families who lived in slum dwellings on the polluted banks of the Sabarmati River had had their homes and lives destroyed in the disaster. A new village was built for survivors on a derelict site seven kilometres outside the industrial city of Ahmedabad. It was called Juhapura. Now this small community is known to people all over the world because of the wonderful work of Mr. Purwar.

I spend the next five days witnessing the magnetic charisma of this noble, humble man who inspires children and parents alike with his incorruptible integrity, respect for his pupils and tireless devotion to the endless quest of creativity. In being given the opportunity to express themselves in all sorts of ways, not only through art, music, dance and craft, but also in conversation, cooking and shopping, cleaning and hygiene, the children are learning for life itself.

They are encouraged to find and develop their own individual strengths and potential and to use them for the benefit of the whole community. The imaginative greetings cards, that the children make, are sold to finance outings and treats, like a picnic at a nature reserve or ice creams from the village shop. Any money left over is saved in a special bank, run by the children themselves, and used to help their families in times of illness and other difficulties.

One small, dilapidated building, without a door in the open entrance and two large trees are the only shelters provided for the Centre but even during the torrential rains of last summer these indomitable children made over two thousand greeting cards. They used their scanty clothes as umbrellas by holding out skirts, scarves and shirts over their creations.

Courage, will power, joy and boundless enthusiasm exude from their frail little bodies infecting my own fragility with new hope. Like all the so-called 'poor' people I have met, they ply me with gifts. A priceless picture of a black elephant walking in a forest, a paper collage ingeniously made from scrap materials, a brightly decorated rosette for my hair and best of all, an expanding newspaper tree which seems to glow with all the colours of the rainbow. My heart leaps within me, as I feel an inexplicable sense of destiny and purpose.

I promise to help them realise their dream of reaching out to all the children of the world through the Spirit of Creativity. I do not know when, I do not know where and I do not know how this dream can come true, but at this moment I share the belief of these little Indian children that it most certainly will.

And now, as I prepare to leave this amazing country, I am unable to capture in words what has been planted in me. It is growing all the time, like a tree from a tiny seed. Flourishing, blossoming, giving, falling, dying and being continuously restored into new life like Creation itself. The sense of the sacred which pervades every aspect of daily life, the imaginative creativity which transforms many a pig's ear into a silk purse, the harmonious communion with the cycles of Nature and above all, the generosity of those who have nothing to give but themselves has made a profound impression on me.

November 23, 1988, is the day of departure. I am in a state of bemused exhaustion when I finally sink into my seat on the plane. I am full of questions but there is also an undeniable conviction that the answers are within my emerging self. I feel ageless and hollow.

I fly home on my fifty third birthday. Am I older or younger, I wonder?
I am in air, in space, out of time; I am so full and yet, so empty
One by one, the bubbles from the bottom of myself rise to the surface
And pause, motionless, for a moment of eternity.
They burst into nothingness, exploding the transparency of my weakness
With the dazzling light of Truth.
I am a mere shadow, grey with poverty
But regardless of my helpless body and dragging spirit,
You step inside my shell,
Showing yourself in all your radiant splendour;
And when I see the glow reflected in their faces
I know that Your flame is still alive in my ashes.

Chapter Nine

LEAP TO FREEDOM

The culture shock hit her the minute she stepped off the plane at Heathrow Airport. The waste was all around her, a half eaten sandwich, discarded plastic cups littering an abandoned table, and an unfinished packet of crisps which nearly had her running after the owner crying, 'Excuse me, I think you must have forgotten these!'

She felt as if she had been taken by the hand to the other side of the world and shown it from a completely different angle. Britain shrank to a small speck of land which no longer seemed very great. Everything she had been taught, told or had assumed was the status quo, was otherwise. Her whole point of view had changed. The cobwebs of illusion, which had clouded her outlook for over half a century, had been swept away leaving a gaping sense of dismay. Susie was overcome by a wave of outrage, guilt, shame and resentment. How could she have been kept in the darkness of ignorance for so long? She entered into, what her daughter called 'an awkward phase', rebelling against the establishment with all the passion of the adolescence she had never had. It had not occurred to the teenage ballet dancer to concern herself with the outside world. The trouble now was that this was not a phase out of which she would grow and the affluent comfort of her life had become very uncomfortable since returning from India.

Susie tried to put her plan to move to Scotland into action as soon as she returned from India. She still hoped to find a small cottage where she could live simply in the uncluttered style that attracted her so much. She scooped up the suitcases, the spinning wheel and the small, brown dog and found rented accommodation near Crieff, to act as a base while she resumed her search for a suitable property to purchase. But after six weeks of intensive but fruitless attempts, the lease ran out and she had to admit defeat again. She returned shame faced to the Isle of Wight with her baggage unpacked. It was not time to go yet, the last act of the marriage had still to be played out.

It had been explained to Susie, by one of her Indian friends, that she would never be free to leave her husband until she had paid off her 'Karmic account'. This meant that any overdraft of guilt, blame, pity and shame had to be cleared, like an outstanding debt, before the next step could open up. She had to take full responsibility for her own decisions and allow her husband to make his in his own way. Only then could they move forward in the spirit of love and forgiveness and out of the present state of deadlock. Whether that would be together or alone was yet to unfold.

Although the 'Karmic account' stuff seemed nonsense to him, the husband no longer took his wife's continuing presence for granted. Susie's reckless trip to India had shaken both of them and they agreed to make one final effort to save their marriage. They flirted with a dream of retirement, where each imagined the other would turn into what he and she wanted, without having to change in themselves. Their mutual aim was to retrieve the happy summer holiday memories that still remained in the pages of their minds like faded snap shots in an old photograph album. He promised to do his best to achieve his long held aim and sell off the business thus allowing the mill house to be turned back into the home it used to be; she promised to support him in making lunch for, and being charming to potential buyers, allowing him to have breakfast meetings with his solicitor and not complaining about the constant influx of strangers into and around the house. They both tried hard to achieve their aim but at the end of the year, when push came to shove, he chose the business and she chose freedom.

The end came about suddenly and in a quite unexpected way. Susie had become a bore about India with her endless talk of 'the sacredness of life' and other such fanciful platitudes like 'the riches of poverty', 'the joy of creativity' and 'the freedom of simplicity'. After one particularly long and animated account about the Children's Creativity Centre, that was of little interest or relevance to the residents of one of England's greenest and most pleasant spots, someone said, 'If you care so much about Indian children why don't you go to Tower Hamlets? There's plenty of them there.'

There had been a lot in the press lately about the plight of the Bangladeshi Community in this poor part of London where many children of homeless immigrant families were without school places. It had not occurred to Susie that she could be of any use there but now the idea had been voiced it stuck in her mind. She decided to investigate the situation.

After making a few enquiries, she was invited to visit a Primary School in Spitalfields, temporarily housed above an adult education centre. Contrary to what Susie had been led to expect, the teachers were not slouched in sullen despondency, but were a group of dedicated and courteous men and women who welcomed her enthusiastically. They had, by their own personal efforts, transformed the top floor of the old building into a light, bright and homely school for about a hundred Bangladeshi children. The youngsters were as polite and cheerful as their teachers and immediately made the white, middle-class stranger feel at home. They listened patiently while she apologised for her lack of youth, strength and maths 'O' level and said none of that mattered if she was willing to give them a hand. Susie agreed to travel up from the Isle of Wight for two days of every week to assist the overworked teachers in any way she could. At first she thought it was only a temporary arrangement but eventually it became clear that this was the Way Out. At last she had something to do and somewhere to go when the last door closed on the future of her marriage.

Thus it was that when the final parting of the ways came on October 4, 1989, exactly a year to the day since she had made her first leap to freedom, Susie leapt again. This time she landed not on the other side of the world but in Tower Hamlets. It was still a long way from Scotland, but at least it was nearer than India.

At first a kind friend put her up in the basement of her large Hampstead house, but the trek from N W 3 to E 1 was just not practicable. Besides, the legacy from her maiden aunt was rapidly diminishing. Susie had to find some more permanent means of supporting herself. Her daughter had suggested trying to apply for the Enterprise Grant and suggested that she might be able to set up a spinning and knitting business. It was a long shot of an idea but there were few other options open to a burnt out ballet teacher with poor health and no other useful qualifications.

Susie was not prepared for the tangled webs of red tape which seemed specially designed to trip up the unwary just when they were at their most vulnerable. She spent hour after hour waiting in crowded, smoky rooms filled with rows of dejected people who stared unseeing into grey space or down at grimy, workless hands. An air of hopeless resignation drenched them with a heavy silence. Numerous forms demanded to know every detail of her non-existent private life and deprived her of any freedom to make decisions about her own future. She was just one more statistic to feed the system. No one seemed to care about any one else, everyone was out for what they could get. Money was all that mattered. Without it you were of no consequence, no use, no value, just one more economic failure. The isolation of person from person frightened her. Never in all the extreme poverty and squalor in India had she experienced such despair or human degradation. Poverty is despised in affluent Britain so the poor very quickly become despicable even to themselves.

The Enterprise Grant turned out not an option because although the ballet teacher had been unable to work (due to ill health) for five years, she had not claimed unemployment benefit. This was a compulsory requirement in order to receive any further assistance from the Department of Social Security. All right, so she'd sign on then. But even this had its problems.

A few weeks after she had finally managed to join the ranks of the unemployed, Susie's newly opened file was abruptly closed. It had not been mentioned that it was forbidden to be sick until she tried to sign on a day later than usual because she had been confined to bed the previous week. Even armed with a sick note from her doctor, she was still struck off the list without warning.

'If you are not fit to sign on' she was told, 'you are not fit to work'.

The only thing left, apparently, was Income Support. Although she had no income to support, Auntie George's money became a stumbling block. The modest sum was not enough to live on but it was above the amount of savings allowed by the Government. What could she do?

The answer came, as always, in an unexpected form.

While looking for a room to rent, Susie discovered a tiny flat for sale on the third floor of a crumbling pre-war block. It had not occurred to her that she could or should buy a property in this extremely undesirable part of London or that there would be anything within her very limited means, but this might solve some of the current problems. She set to work to see if she could raise enough money to put in an offer. Everything that could be was sold, a few shares, insurance policies, jewellery and some furniture but she still had to beg a small advance from her mother's will before the required amount could be scraped together. The offer Susie put in was immediately accepted. There was no competition for city pads in Spitalfields at this time. It was before the old fruit market was converted for leisure activities and Sunday shopping and the area became fashionable. The estate agent was delighted to find someone gullible enough to fall for his euphemistic sales talk and the delusion of space and light in the small flat, created by a hastily applied layers of thick, magnolia paint.

It was a tight schedule to assemble the total sum the day before completion but Susie managed to hand over the final cheque to her solicitor the day before 'Move In'.

So there she was, at 8a.m. on February 16, 1990, sitting on the floor of her new home, on a pile of dustbin liners containing her few belongings. At last all the hurry and hassle was over and all that was left to be done, was to wait for the gasman and the electrician to come and connect her to those services. She had even remembered to inform the correct offices of her move so there was nothing more to worry about. Or so she thought.

Her first visitor was unexpected. It was Mr. Michael, the estate agent. He seemed very agitated as, without so much as a 'Good-Morning', he exclaimed, 'You are illegal!'

Susie was somewhat taken aback by this unfriendly greeting. He had always been so charming before.

'The bank hasn't released your cheque yet,' he went on, 'You can't stay here'.

Susie calmly explained that she has nowhere else to go and he could hardly put her out in the street, she was sure the whole thing could be sorted out with a simple telephone call to the bank. Mr. Michael escorted his client briskly down the three flights of stairs to the public telephone in the corner shop, but before they could reach it they bumped into the electrician on his way up. Assuring the estate agent she would contact the bank as soon as she had let the electrician into her flat, Susie retraced her steps with her new visitor. He took one look at the filthy fuse box on the balcony wall, which Susie had not even noticed, and said darkly,

'You've got problems Miss,' his face creased with a worried frown, 'All the fuses have been nicked.' There was worse to come. 'They're non- standard and probably discontinued anyway'.

'Oh,' Susie replied forlornly, 'what can you do?'

'Not a lot, make enquiries to-morrow,' the man muttered non-commitedly.

She watched him retreat down the stairs with helpless resignation, thinking, 'better get on and ring the bank'.

Reaching the ground floor she was astonished to see the electrician standing on a small stepladder, peering intently into the fuse box of an empty flat.

'Got one!' he cried triumphantly. Susie stared, fascinated, as he lugged the ladder up floor by floor, from fuse box to fuse box, repeating this dubious practise on each landing.

'Only one more to go', he seemed to be warming to the challenge but, a few boxes later, he disappeared into the street without a word. Susie's heart sank. Minutes passed before the man returned grinning widely.

'Just happened to find an old fuse lurking in the back of me van,' he grinned.

Susie sighed with relief. 'So now I can have the power on?' she asked hopefully.

'Only up to a point, Miss, the wires are pretty dicey and will have to be replaced before you can risk more than a minimal load.'

'At least I have light' Susie thought, as she waved good-bye to the electrician with many a 'thank you' for all his trouble.

'Better get on and ring the bank,' she muttered, like a repetitive mantra on her next attempt to reach the phone. The gasman met her on the second floor. Susie gently broke it to him that the second hand cooker he had come to connect was in pieces in the boot of her car.

'Can't touch it luv,' he shrugged, 'not with me back.'

Her face fell as he, like the electrician, retreated down the stairs. He looked back and caught sight of the helpless woman still standing in silent dejection.

'What make is it?' he called up to her.

'Dunno' replied Susie, wondering if it mattered, but nevertheless she followed the gasman into the street where her car was parked. They both peered gloomily into the crammed boot at the dismantled cooker, strewn on top of boxes, bundles and baggage.

'Got a pair of gloves?'

This sudden and seemingly bizarre question snapped Susie out of her lost thoughts. She donned her purple woollen mittens without a word. It was a cold morning and she was glad of them. Meanwhile the gasman had got the back of the cooker out of the car and was grasping its two spindly legs. He bade her to take hold of the top.

'What about your back?' Susie didn't dare to mention her own.

He did not reply but continued to struggle doggedly up the stairs without pausing once. Susie had no choice but to struggle weakly behind him, clinging onto her bit of the cooker with grim determination. They were both breathless when they reached the third floor flat and stood gasping and grunting. After a few minutes rest and without a word passing between them Susie and the gasman went back to the car to fetch the rest of the cooker. When the whole painful operation was completed and all the pieces had been dumped upon the floor of the minute kitchen the man examined the connecting pipe. 'That's no good,' he muttered, with the dismissive air of a professional.

'Of course not,' Susie agreed, 'wouldn't be, would it?'

She braced herself for the next problem. Miraculously a new pipe was discovered in the depths of the workman's bulging bag and he proceeded to complete the job in hand.

'Could you possibly connect up the radiators as well please?' Susie dared to ask politely. He shook his head, looking doubtfully at the rusty pipes. 'Can't touch them, luv,' he replied, repeating his opening remark.

Susie was not surprised and decided to make a cup of tea instead of protesting. She watched the gasman running down the stairs with surprising agility. The forty pounds that he had just taken off Susie seemed to have had a remarkable effect on his back. She sighed. She would have one more try at ringing the bank before the next interruption, whatever that might be. She reached the corner shop without delay, and asked permission to use the phone.

'Sorry, dear,' the shopkeeper replied, 'ever since you used it this morning it has been out of order,' adding after a thoughtful pause, 'Funny that.'

Trudging slowly back up to her flat, Susie wondered if she was meant to ring the bank. She was too tired to think and collapsed back onto the dustbin liners with a deep feeling of resignation. 'Whatever happens now', she mused, 'at least I am here.'

The sun still shone through the grimy windows and bathed her in a pool of bright warmth. She had asked the local priest to come along tomorrow to bless her new home but now that no longer seemed necessary. Susie was quite sure that God had already done it. With that reassuring thought she sank into a comforting slumber in the middle of the sunny spot on the floor.

Loud knocking on the door rudely awakened her. It was the Attrils from the Isle of Wight.

They were the family removal firm that Susie had employed to bring up the contents of her spinning shed from her former, to her present, home. Mum, Dad and Bobby burst into the flat exclaiming, 'Oh, ain't it 'orrible,' with cheerful grins all over their healthy country faces. 'Don't know 'ow you can live in a place like this,' they tactlessly went on.

The noise of the traffic-jammed streets, police sirens and car alarms floated through the open door. Susie didn't suppose for an instant that they could understand why anyone in their right senses would exchange the peace of the pretty little island for this. She didn't attempt to explain.

The man, woman and boy unloaded a single bed, two upright chairs, a small table, Susie's mother's desk and a few other articles which completed the extent of her possessions. When these had been deposited beside the dustbin liners it was a relief to let the Attrils return to their rural idyll.

It was now too late to ring the bank so she rang her solicitor from a call box in the next street. Susie was expecting a scolding and was surprised to learn that the errant cheque had been released from the bank hours ago. The solicitor had been in contact with the estate agent and given him a scolding when she discovered the unsatisfactory state of the electricity and gas supplies. It appeared that Susie was entitled to some sort of compensation and that the famous cheque was being withheld until this had been accomplished. This heavily disguised blessing made her think that perhaps everything was going to be all right after all.

* * *

At home, in the sunny box, the woman knows why the next six years had to be spent living in one of the poorest districts of London. It was all part of the invisible pattern that was to piece together the patchwork that became the Rainbow Tree. More than that, the patchwork itself would be the structure upon which Susie built the project that gave new meaning and a sense of purpose to her shattered life. What is now just a bundle of tattered old fabric folded up in a grubby canvas bag lying under the table would soon become the greatest inspiration of Susie's entire life.

Chapter Ten

THE ARTIST WITHIN

In spring 1990 Susie had three things on which to hang her life. In those early days in the East End it was not health nor wealth or a job which gave security and purpose to her existence, but three things of priceless value.

The first was Sophia, the spinning wheel. She came into her own now that Trumpet had had to be left behind on the Isle of Wight and was a more convenient companion than a small brown dog for a woman living alone in an inner city flat. It may have seemed a strange sight to some to see Susie walking in the streets of London with Sophia slung onto her shoulder by means of a guitar strap, and sometimes in the park with all the dog owners. The spinning wheel gave the lone woman confidence to sit outside and spin when the weather was fine. It gave her something to do, something to talk about with passers by or, more often, stoppers to chat. Everyone seemed to have a granny or an auntie in Ireland or Lithuania, Canada or India who used to sit and spin like Susie. Sophia was a great source of fascinating conversations and did not run off to chase ducks when let off her guitar strap.

The second thing was being with children. Susie became a child again, cutting out and colouring in with the Bangladeshi children in Spitalfields and the multicultural Britons in the Isle of Dogs. She found herself in demand since not many people had time to lend a free hand to the heavily burdened teachers in the East End. The curriculum allowed little time for play, a vital part of any child's development, and even craft was on the decline due to the aggressive advance of technology. A woman with a spinning wheel was a welcome novelty.

In the crumbling schools squatting underneath the immense shadow of the new Docklands Development Susie encountered a very different kind of deprivation from that of the immigrant community on the other side of the river. These were the indigenous dispossessed. Whole communities had been dismantled and robbed of their way of life when the work of generations of dockers was no longer required. The anger of the parents and grandparents flared up in children who stabbed each other with pencils without knowing why. Perhaps it was the sight of high and mighty office windows looking disdainfully down upon the broken panes in pre-war council houses, or the closure of the pristine Docklands Light Railway on Friday nights when the businessmen left for their country cottages that incensed those who were denied the privilege of using it at weekends. (Later, this omission was rectified and it is now possible to travel to Greenwich and the Tower of London on Saturdays and Sundays as well as weekdays). The divisions of this unfair society seemed much more complex than Susie had been led to believe and her perception was changing rapidly. But children were children wherever they lived and she longed to find a way of linking them together, free from the barriers and labels imposed upon them.

The third thing was completely unexpected. St. James' Piccadilly was unlike any other church which Susie had ever encountered. Drama, music, art and even dance were encouraged to bring alive the traditional religious festivals in innovative ways. Despite the physical frailty which bellied her professional background, she joined the liturgical dance group when some kind person told her, 'we take anyone. You don't have to be a dancer!'

The St. James' community included many who, like Susie, were on spiritual journeys and had left previous life-styles behind. They became friends and often spent the whole day together on Sundays. They had plenty of time to stay and chat over lunch in the adjoining café, no one being in a hurry to go back to drab bed sitters, empty flats and lonely hostels. There were a wide variety of activities to join like lessons on the Indian scriptures, a singing group, art and music workshops and creative meditation. It was wonderful to find such a lively and interesting church where everyone was welcome and the doors seldom closed.

Susie soon became involved in several different ways and found new outlets for old skills. These awakened the artist hidden within the former choreographer and performer. She was especially interested in the theatrical portrayal of religious events. Inspired by the images so vividly described in Biblical accounts, she painted a striking back cloth called 'the Shadow of the Cross' and transformed the altar with vivid saris, bought in the East End, for a dance-drama at St. James Church at Easter 1991.

The radical rector declared that the painting made a powerful symbolic statement and invited her to make a series of altar hangings to mark some of the other major events in the Christian Calendar. Susie leapt at the opportunity with customary enthusiasm despite her lack of knowledge about textile art. She turned the biggest of her three small rooms into a studio. Huge pieces of calico, bought in wholesale fabric shops, were laid out on the floor and the local market turned out to be a wonderful source of cheap art materials. Everything the budding artist needed was near at hand including a course on 'Creative Textiles' at the local college.

By the end of 1991, Susie had created four more large works for the feasts of the Baptism of Christ, Pentecost, the Transfiguration of the Lord and All Soul's and All Saint's. All of these were used in worship at St. James on the relevant occasions. By the end of November there was only one of the series left to make.

To spend Christmas on the holy Isle of Iona had long been a desire of Susie's. She had discovered this magical place, off the West Coast of Scotland, during a recent holiday and had vowed then not to leave before finding a cottage to rent for the month of December. The converted steading of an old farmhouse was the only accommodation available at that time but what could be more suitable than to spend Christmas in an old cattle shed?

The image for the final 'visionary altar hanging' took the form of a radiant seed bursting through the broken husk of an old tree. It was inspired by the evocative poetry in the book of Isaiah chosen for the festival of Epiphany.

Soon it became difficult to work in the rented quarters so Susie sought a bigger space in which to spread out the large hanging. The warden of Iona Abbey listened to the artist's request for a work area and surprised her by offering the floor of the sacred church building itself. Thus it was that Susie spent most of Christmas week kneeling on the ancient, cold, stone flags painting a symbol of light at the darkest time of the year. Whenever she was asked what she was doing she would answer, 'I am an artist in prayer'.

When she returned to London and showed her work to the rector he invited her to mount an exhibition of the complete series at St. James' Church. The six hangings told a story of light moving through the eternal annual cycle, bringing life out of death and hope out of despair.

The choreographer's overall eye saw that something was needed to link them together in a cohesive way. Movement, music and dramatic readings would give added dimension to the visual images. Susie had no trouble in finding talented friends among the congregation who were willing to take part. Together they presented a unique unveiling ceremony and celebration for the opening of the exhibition on August 6, 1992.

Although she still suffered from bouts of chronic fatigue and painful spinal inflammation, the spirit of the dancer was being restored. If dance was the language of the soul then she was learning different ways with words and phrases that gave her strength even on the days when she could not get out of bed. Sometimes she would be plunged into helpless desolation and a depth of loneliness where nothing existed but pain. But even then, something new was coming to life within her.

The seed of an idea had been planted in Susie in India three years ago. She had been back to the Children's Creativity Centre the previous winter to learn more about the unique way all forms of creative expression were used to develop self confidence and communication skills in the deprived children of Ahmedabad. She had even managed to arrange to bring some of the Indian teachers to Britain by persuading her educational contacts on the Isle of Wight to employ them to give workshops in a few schools there. Her own services were given on a purely voluntary basis and the travel expenses covered by a backlog from Susie's income support plus the annual Christmas gift from her mother.

This was the format that was to establish the whole of the vast Educational Arts Project which eventually grew out of these humble beginnings.

* * *

It is the day after the Winter Solstice in December 2001. The woman in the sunny box pauses to take a look through the window of time. The perspective has changed. She can see further than Susie could when the idea of the Rainbow Tree was just beginning to take shape in her mind. The clarity of the vision is enhanced by the distance of the years and the image of a five-pointed star set in the centre of a tree shines brightly as the light begins to return to the Northern Hemisphere.

The Rainbow Tree has four branches and a huge triangular trunk in the spaces between the five brilliant points. The top two are the spiritual branches of Susie's life in the Far East and the near West. The centre two are the sources of her creativity branching out in new directions, the trunk is the life she is growing out of and the star is the point she is reaching towards. It connects the past, present and future and gives the branches a symmetry into which they all fit beautifully.

The star shines with the seven colours of the rainbow and hanging around it are seven large seeds. Inside each is an element of creation.

The Purple seed holds the planets of space;
The Indigo seed holds creatures of the sea;
The Blue seed holds birds of the air;
The Green seed holds plants of the earth;
The Yellow seed holds animals of the wild;
The Orange seed holds peoples of the world;
And from the Red seed flows a never-ending stream of hope.

The woman takes a closer look at the vision.

The seeds are moving now, weaving the pattern of a dance, intermingling the colours without losing their own unique quality. The true nature of each seed penetrates her consciousness creating an intense sensory impression. She can taste the essence of the hidden fruit concealed in the coloured seeds.

Purple is sharp and sour, the taste of grief, of mourning the end of a marriage.
Indigo is overpowering, bringing tears to her eyes and upsetting her insides.
Blue is cool, as swirling emotions cease, the taste of loneliness becomes calm.
Green is wholesome, the raw taste of fresh growth, new energy and healing.
Yellow is as rich as honey with the bitter after-taste of the forbidden fruit.
Orange is sweet, refreshing the soul who has wandered in the wilderness.
Red is a warm, comforting taste flooding the whole body with lasting goodness.

The seeds drop, one by one onto the rich, dark earth. Rain begins to fall, softening the outer shells gently. They crack and open and spill the contents into the receptive, merciful soil. The tiny fragments of life will sleep in the womb of Susie's mind until spring awakens them.

Then, the woman will once again open the door of the sunny box and feel the energy motivating the planets, see the movement dancing on the sea and the light reflecting the scudding clouds and hear the calling birds across the distant fields as darkness recedes over the hills.

She begins to realise that the Rainbow Tree is both the Tree of life and the Tree of Knowledge integrating the painful steps of growth that have brought her home.

Chapter Eleven

THE RAINBOW TREE

The idea of the Rainbow Tree came to Susie in September 1993 but it was another nine months before it would grow into its completed form. It was so much more than a vast patchwork made in five separate sections by children who had previously been unaware of each other's existence. It was the belief in what they were doing that held the groups together and wove an underlying network of trust sustaining the whole project. Right from the start they had no doubt that they were creating a fabric of friendship that would embrace children all over the world. Whether they lived in India, the Isle of Wight, Tower Hamlets, London or Iona, whether their skin was black, white or brown or their feet barefoot or shod in the latest trainers it made no difference. All the children shared the vision of the Rainbow Tree. What mattered was the opportunity for each child to express his unique ideas in a completely original way within the overall design they were creating together.

Susie told the children that every one of us is born into this world with the potential to become a talented and joyful human being. Like a birthday present within us, she said, the parcel of our special gift may have to be passed around the circles of life many times before its inner treasure is unwrapped, but when the music stops, (as it had for wee Susie) we often need someone to help us to undo the knots.

The Rainbow Tree would help to undo the knots of uncertainty and inhibition and reconnect the children to the source of their own and each other's inborn creativity.

Susie saw the opportunity to link the five groups of children with whom she was already connected through different aspects of her life.

A tree of friendship could bring together those she worked with in the inner-city schools of Spitalfields and the Isle of Dogs and the eleven children of the tiny island school of Iona. The link could be set up during the month of September when Susie and her spinning wheel had volunteered for the post of craft worker for the Iona Community. Also, she had been seeking a way to develop the link between schools on the Isle of Wight and the Indian children since their teachers' visit the previous year. This was it. This was the purpose she had been seeking. It seemed like a God given task for which she had been gradually and systematically prepared. All she had to do now was simply to go to each of the five different groups and invite the children to make a branch of the Rainbow Tree.

Susie set out to design a large patchwork. Unbleached calico, readily available and cheap to buy in the wholesale fabric stores near her flat would form the basis of the work. She cut out five triangles of cloth. Each measured seven feet by six feet by six feet, six inches, a calculation that could only have been invented by a ballet dancer unhindered by the restrictions of a mathematical education.

Iona Primary School was the first to receive a section of the Rainbow Tree. The craft worker spent her day off helping the children to make their branch. Apart from the blank piece of fabric, every stage of the work was executed and designed by the children themselves. The colour of the painted background, the texture of the branches and the leaves of friendship made in the shape of their hands were all their own ideas. Every pupil of Iona Primary School, from wee Stuart, aged five, to big Keith, aged eleven, cut, sewed, decorated and wrote their names on the first branch of the famous patchwork tree.

When Susie returned to London at the beginning of October she repeated this process with the Bangladeshi and Docklands children who made their own very different branches. There was just time to set up the making of the huge trunk in a Middle school on the Isle of Wight before the trip to India. The older children here were keen to try the uninhibited methods of creativity demonstrated by teachers from the Creativity Centre and they quite literally painted the bark by hand. Many hands smeared with a delicious mixture of thick green, red, black and brown paints, enjoyed a rare messy treat they thought they had left behind at Primary school.

The question of how to sew the finished branches and trunk together now arose. Encouraged by the enthusiastic response to her idea, Susie planned to find a way of gathering a few children from each of the five groups together to assemble the patchwork when it was completed. With this in mind she set off to India, vowing to try to arrange for two children from Ahmedabed to bring their branch to London next summer. This was to prove even more difficult to organise than the teachers' visit the previous year and the whole of Susie's Christmas present from her mother went to pay the fares. But everyone, from visa officer, passport official and immigration authorities to a reporter from the Indian Times, got caught up in the excitement and permission was finally granted. The Rainbow Tree and all the children who made the Indian branch were famous by the time Susie's six-week visit came to an end and she was able to return to London assured that everything was in place for the summer Assembly.

So it was that in June 1994, Vijay aged nine and Farzana aged twelve, accompanied by two women teachers and Mr. Purwar, embarked on a momentous journey to London. Never in their wildest dreams had the two village children imagined travelling on the over night train from Ahmedabad to Bombay, let alone flying in a jumbo jet to the other side of the world. Entrusted to carry the precious branch, Vijay and Farzana were aware of the unprecedented importance of their mission. They were on their way to meet up with the English, Scottish, Bangladeshi and London children to unite the pieces of the Rainbow Tree at the very first Festival of Friendship.

The head quarters were situated at Susie's tiny flat. Neil and Gavin had travelled from Iona with wee Stuart's Mum and Sapphire and Tash came up from the Isle of Wight to join the Indians in week of creative friendship. Susie had said as long as no one was more than five feet long they would fit into her ten feet sitting room. They had to sleep end to end and pack their sleeping bags away every morning to make a space for breakfast but that was all part of the fun.

Each day started with a unique blend of prayers. The three boys, three girls, two Indian women, the Scottish Mum, Mr. Purwar and Paul from next door, Susie and her new flat mate Lucy all gathered together round a candle set in the middle of the square room. Hindu chants and Alleluias united with praises to Allah and a Celtic blessing to make one seamless hymn. Susie was beginning to realise that God's House had indeed room for all His children to live happily together whether they had done their homework on time or not.

After breakfast the resident group set out every morning from the bulging seams of the third floor flat, to meet up with children from the two London schools. They had been lent workshop space at Spitalfields Old Marketplace. The little procession wove its way along the crowded East End streets carrying all manner of equipment for the day's activities. Not only did these entail sewing together the branches and trunk of the giant tree but also included music, dance, drumming, songs, costume making and most important of all, a picnic lunch.

Shared meals were an essential part of the Festival. Each evening, on returning to the flat, food from a different country was prepared and sampled. The children were in charge of the menu, shopping for ingredients on the way home and presiding over the cooking. Adults were willing helpers in the making of moong bean curry, baked tatties and stovies, Mars Bar sauce and the universally popular chips.

At last the day of the Festival arrived. The final stitch had been put into the vast patchwork. The completed Rainbow Tree measured sixteen by fourteen feet. Its magnificence exceeded their greatest expectations and its huge size surprised everyone. It seemed to have grown in the past week and the only place high and wide enough to display it was the brand new toilet block in the centre of the Market

Place. The flat roof made an ideal stage for the multicultural songs and dances bursting forth from the elated group.

Soon a small crowd gathered to join in the celebrations. The brilliantly coloured, many-facetted textile collage infected young and old alike with its special magic. From the beginning it had a life of its own but no one could have guessed, on that June Sunday in 1994, that this was only the first of many Festivals of Friendship or that the Rainbow Tree would grow into a seven-year venture of faith with branches all over the world.

The final stage of the celebrations was yet to come. A special service of blessing had been arranged to welcome the Rainbow Tree to Iona Abbey where it would reside for the next four months. The huge patchwork was folded and rolled and squashed until it fitted into the biggest laundry bag that could be found. It was then duly taken to the home of Neil and Gavin who proudly escorted their Indian friends on the twelve hour long journey by train, ferry, bus and another smaller ferry to the tiny island of Iona. An eager party greeted the travellers and their precious cargo as they clambered up the slippery slope of the jetty to fall into waiting arms of welcome. The two Scottish boys were immediately engulfed by their families while the rest of the group were escorted to accommodation in one of the Community Guest houses. Relief at the safe arrival and accomplishment of so many hopes soon overwhelmed excitement. It was not long before everyone was fast asleep.

Next morning the laundry bag revealed the full extent of its treasure. Laid out upon the same cold, stone floor where Susie had knelt to paint the giant seed containing the Light of the World, the vibrant tree seemed to fill the whole place. An emergency meeting was hastily called by the Abbey trustees to discuss where, when and how to hang the huge textile. Special permission had to be obtained in order to allow several stout nails to be discreetly knocked into the sacred walls of the listed building. Workmen with ladders and hammers took over proceedings and Susie sat back imagining that her God given task had been completed.

At last the Rainbow Tree was in place. Its stunning presence made an immediate impact on all the many visitors to the famous abbey but none were more eager to see it than the pupils of Iona Primary School. At ten minutes to three precisely a great rush of children burst through the imposing grey stone doorway and ran up to their masterpiece with eager anticipation. Agog, in the first instant, to locate their own particular leaf or the exact section of bark they had personally made, they then stood back in utter amazement to stare at the immensity of the whole hanging. Susie had been right. Even although the island on which they lived was very small they had become part of something very big.

Their dream had come true. Now they knew that all children everywhere could be friends and make their shared world a beautiful place.

They had been preparing the service of blessing and to welcome their Indian visitors for many days. Now the big moment had come at last. Neil and Gavin gave the opening speech. 'We travelled to London to meet our friends, Vijay and Farzana, who have come all the way from India to be with us here to-day,' they said.

'At the Festival of Friendship we learned about each other's cultures and lives, shared food and games, stories and songs and sewed the Rainbow Tree together. This banner began in five different places but now it has become One as we ourselves have all become one group. To-day, we want to celebrate our togetherness and remember that God loves us all no matter where we come from.'

Then everyone joined their voices in saying, 'May every leaf of the Rainbow Tree be a friendship shared across the world, may every branch be a resting place for understanding and every root strengthen the commitment we have made to caring for and respecting each other. May our lives bear the fruits of the Spirit of Hope and Harmony that brought us together in this great venture of Faith.'

The fruits that the tree bore that summer of 1994 were greater than anyone expected. The beacon of light that had shone from the shores of Iona for hundreds of years shone particularly brightly that year. After the recent dismantling of the Berlin Wall there was a flood of visitors from Eastern Europe coming to the holy island on spiritual pilgrimages. The Rainbow Tree in Iona Abbey spoke of a peace and friendship at this time when a stream of new hope had been released into the world.

It seemed that Susie's task was just beginning. Invitations from Poland, Prague and a tiny village in North East Germany pressed her to take the tree of friendship to those countries. It seemed that many more children were out there just waiting to join this exciting new project. Offers of free accommodation and introductions to schools were hard to resist. There seemed no choice but to gratefully accept.

The fruits of imagination were already dropping seeds into the fertile ground of the former choreographer's mind. Like the woman in the box she sees seven seeds of seven colours spreading out over a seven years. A vision of a fantastic textile exhibition made by children all over the world began to take shape. This would be their gift to the world for the new Millennium in the year 2001.

Time was beginning to catch up with itself. The beginning and the end were already linked. The complete design was contained within the mother tree before she was once again folded up into the bag like a giant seed herself.

Waiting for the last branch of The Rainbow Tree to arrive from Iona, and,
below, the complete tree with some of its creators – 1994, London

The Elements – Purple Year 1994/95

The Planets – Purple Year 1994/95

Water Works – Indigo Year 1995/96

Aquatic Life – Indigo Year 1995/96

iii

Wind, Clouds and Sky – Blue Year 1996/97

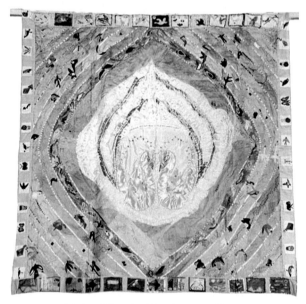

Birds of Travel – Blue Year 1996/97

Our Shared Earth – Green Year 1997/98

Green and Growing – Green Year 1997/98

Deserts and Mountains – Yellow Year 1998/99

Wild Animals – Yellow Year 1998/99

House of Many Dwellings – Orange Year 1999/2000

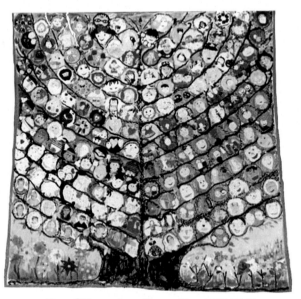

Tree of Humanity – Orange Year 1999/2000

Red Ray of Hope – Cartmel Priory, 2000

The Rainbow Tree – Cartmel Priory, 2000

Chapter Twelve

HAVE TREE, WILL TRAVEL

It was quite a year, 1995. The Rainbow Tree and Susie travelled to Poland, Prague, North East Germany, India and Russia before the year was out.

The first port of call was the home of Yola Sarni in the small town of Nowy Sacz in Northern Poland. Yola had met Susie in Iona when they were both volunteers for the Community in 1994. The Polish teacher invited the craft worker to bring the huge patchwork to the 'special needs' school where she worked. As a result Susie set off from Waterloo station on a fine June morning, armed with a railway ticket to Warsaw, the large laundry bag and a small rucksack.

The long journey involved an overnight stay in Brussels, a change of train at the big, bustling station of Warsaw and not a few anxious moments. But sure enough when the final destination was safely reached there was Yola waiting, just as Susie remembered her, with a wide grin all over her face. As soon as the two friends were re-united it was as if they had never been apart. All doubts and worries were instantly dissolved in their joyous tears of welcome. It was all so simple. The strength of their trust had stretched out like a length of rope between them giving the intrepid traveller something to cling onto all the way from London.

Yola's flat was even smaller than Susie's. It only had one room with a sofa and chair that converted into beds at night. There was a tiny cooking area and a bathroom cunningly squeezed into the entrance passage. Both were squeaky clean and showed the same fastidious tidiness that gave the whole place an ordered peace.

The concrete block was surrounded by open land and looked across at neighbouring apartments, but despite the stark appearance of the complex there was an air of friendliness. Youngsters of all ages, from toddlers to teenagers, played happily and safely together in a communal respect, which would now seem old fashioned in modern Britain. As would the seams in women's stockings, the pinafores they wore to do their housework and the old men puffing clay pipes on the flower-filled balconies. The homely atmosphere and simple life style was comforting to Susie but Yola longed for a bigger flat and a washing machine.

Next morning they took the trolley bus to the school. What must the children have thought when the small grey haired woman entered their classroom dragging behind her what seemed like a large bag of washing? No doubt Yola had told them about the Rainbow Tree project but the surprise on all those young faces widened when they were bidden to open the laundry bag.

Then the magic happened.

Twenty square metres of vibrant colour spilled out to cover the whole floor. Gasps of amazement filled the air with incredulous excitement. Susie and Yola stood still and watched the reaction of the children. They understood immediately. Without hesitation they knelt down and covered the leaf-shaped hands with their own, seeming to feel the energy with which they had been made and hearing the silent language of the Rainbow Tree. No words were needed to explain the messages of hope that it bore. Instantaneous as touch, the bonds of friendship had already been woven across the world like roots under the sea.

The Polish children wasted no time in responding. Before long, paper, pens and scissors were distributed so that they could draw round, cut out, decorate and embellish their own hands of friendship. These were then glued to the branches of the magic tree, squeezing between English and Indian ones, overlapping Scottish ones and interlinking with the Bangladeshis. There was no doubt that a new Polish branch had been securely grafted onto the Rainbow Tree.

Yola's class eagerly accepted Susie's invitation to take part in the next stage of the Project, a new series of patchworks entitled 'The Rainbow Seeds'. The first pair was linked to the colour purple and depicted the themes of energy and space. Energy took the form of 'The Elements' and space the form of 'The Planets'. The former had already been completed earlier in the year but the latter had yet to be started. Susie suggested that the Polish children could embroider a section of 'The Planets' border with 'Stars of Hope'. This two-metre strip of purple cotton could easily be posted to London when it was completed and then be joined it to the other sections in due course. She had designed these smaller patchworks to be peripatetic from the start unlike the cumbersome original! It was becoming increasingly difficult to squash the enlarged Rainbow Tree back into its bag but with much pushing and shoving, laughing and shouting the zip was finally coaxed over the last bulge and the heavy load strapped once more upon the travel trolley.

Susie's next stop was Prague. Skola Zakladni Sporilov was very different from the humble Polish boarding school. Smart desks replaced hand carved benches and rustic tables, there were double glazed windows instead of home made curtains and not a macramé pot holder was in sight. The Czech children exuded sophisticated city confidence and the dashing young headmaster welcomed his unusual visitor with practised charm. Anna, Susie's hostess was also sophisticated. The smart, efficient business woman bore little resemblance to the dishevelled pilgrim who had visited Iona last year. Only her dancing eyes belied her cool exterior as she tried to explain the purpose of Susie's mission. Mr. Daniel Kayser was intrigued. He bade the two women to follow him into the main hall where a group of teenagers was waiting expectantly.

It happened again.

Colour magically burst out of the shabby bag like a giant butterfly emerging from a chrysalis. It hardly seemed possible that more hands could be pressed upon the crowded branches, more names inscribed upon the huge trunk, but these youngsters were determined. Their symbols of friendship were works of art. Beautifully drawn and carefully painted scenes of happy horses, sumptuous sunsets, fantastic flowers and doves of peace adorned hands, hearts and exotically shaped leaves.

The international Rainbow Tree was displayed in the entrance of the school for all to see until it was time for the ritual of re-packing. The second section of the 'Stars of Hope' gave the children something to hold onto when Susie left. It linked the growing family and connected them to each other in a realistic and tangible way. If seeing was believing then touching was for real. In sharing the work of their hands all the children were quite literally in touch with each other.

Susie's third hostess was an eccentric young woman minister in the Lutheran Church. Her parish, the tiny village of Gielow, was tucked away deep in the forests of North East Germany. After an arduous journey this peaceful oasis was like a paradise far removed from traffic and noisy streets. The minister lived in a large, rambling old house with many rooms. There were several guests, besides Susie, all of whom seemed perfectly at home and the atmosphere was relaxed and friendly. A spacious and luxurious bedroom with self-contained bathroom was put at her disposal.

Next morning the Sunday school children were summoned to add their marks to the flourishing tree. The excitement was great. They danced and sang and played and prayed that the hopes of little children would unite all people like the stars on the border and that the leaves of the tree would be for the healing of the nations.

Just like it said in the Bible.

It was with mixed feelings that Susie hauled the huge and precious cargo back to London. Sad to leave, glad to have completed her mission, hopeful for the future of the project but fearful of her ability to cope with the growing potential. The laundry bag was now too big to fit into the luggage racks of the various trains and buses and kept falling off the trolley it had outgrown. There was no way she could ever do this again, thought Susie, imagining that the travels of the Rainbow Tree were over.

How wrong she was.

* * *

Back in her little flat, Susie collapsed thankfully into bed. She stayed there for three days. Then the telephone rang. Some one she barely remembered, from a workshop some months ago, was asking her if she wanted to meet some Russian teachers.

'Not now', Susie sighed, 'I've just got back from Eastern Europe and I'm exhausted.'

'They are only here for a week on a course at Enfield College and I've told them about your friendship project,' the voice came back. 'An educational psychologist from Moscow University wants to meet you.'

Weakly, Susie agreed to go to a meeting the following day. She set off with reluctance, hastily gathering a few photographs and hand written leaflets about last year's festival. There had been no time to prepare and her mind was as tired as her body. She had little idea what to say to such eminent professors.

It was the lunch break when she arrived. The teacher who had rung Susie hurried into the college restaurant where a group of severe looking men and women were conversing in rapid Russian in between mouthfuls of macaroni cheese.

'Please explain your project as briefly and clearly as possible,' Susie was told by the interpreter, 'we do not have much time to spare.'

Shuffling the photographs and pieces of paper around uncomfortably, she tried to convey the spirit of her unconventional venture and the hopes to link children of different countries together. When asked if it was supported by the British Government Susie could only shake her head sadly. She felt she had failed completely to impress these important Russians and was taken aback when one said, 'You will be contacted.'

'By the K.G.B. no doubt,' Susie thought gloomily.

The next day the telephone rang again. 'Alloa', the caller cried loudly, as if from the other side of the world. 'Here is Yelena Sukhova. To-morrow I come to Liverpool.'

'Street Station?' Susie tentatively enquired.

'Da, da da, yes that is correct,' laughed Yelena. She sounded quite jolly for a K.G.B. officer.

'I will wear my yellow trouser suit so that you will recognise me,' Susie was beginning to rise to the challenge.

'And I will wear a shocking pink costume,' retaliated the Russian.

They agreed to meet at the station at ten thirty the following morning. The usual swirling grey mass of hurried, flurried commuters was suddenly interrupted by two bold bursts of colour moving rapidly towards each other. One came running down the stairs from the street, the other alighted from a train full of black-brief-cased businessmen and women oblivious of the momentous meeting that was about to happen. When shocking pink met sunshine yellow it was as if a flame had been set alight. It was one of those inexplicable instances in life when two become one, united in something they do not even know they share. It was as if an invisible energy had simultaneously embraced them both in a moment of instant recognition. Bursting into the laughter of relief, the two women chatted non-stop on the fifteen-minute walk back to Susie's flat.

They felt comfortable together as soon as they entered the unpretentious interior on the third floor of the crumbling block. Later, Susie was to discover that it was not dissimilar from the Russian visitor's own home. The secondary school teacher had joined the delegation at the last moment when her supervisor had suddenly dropped out. As the most junior member, she had been instructed to contact the co-ordinator of the children's friendship project that had failed to interest the higher authorities. It was as much of a relief to the

Russian to discover that Susie was not some intimidating executive, as it was to have her vision of a K.G.B. officer so delightfully shattered. Yelena was as glamorous as a film star and as far removed from an intimidating official as a rose from a grisly bear.

Two hours later, Susie accepted Yelena's invitation to take the Rainbow Tree to her school in Cheboksary. Yelena made her repeat the name CHE-BOK-SARY several times before she was satisfied with the pronunciation. After all, she was a language teacher and spoke English perfectly. This charming and accomplished woman was also very determined. Determined that Susie should come to Russia at Christmas.

'To talk to our children about God,' she said.

How could Susie refuse a request that seemed like a command from on high?

Burying her reservations about confronting the famous Russian winter so soon after the famous Indian summer, - a trip in October was already arranged - she agreed to do what she was asked.

Then Yelena told her how to get there!

The flight to Moscow was the easy part. It was the twelve-hour overnight train journey that concerned the lone traveller. An unaccompanied woman, without a word of Russian, was surely going to have difficulties?

'Don't worry,' Yelena dazzled her irresistible smile. 'Everything will be arranged.'

'Trust me.'

Trust. That was it. That was the invisible energy embracing them both. They had trusted each other instantly, without question, without doubt from the beginning. Trust was the key to the whole thing.

* * *

That key again. It seemed to have less to do with boxes, windows or doors than intangible things like light and trust. The woman is reminded of the famous 'Light of the World' painting by William

Holman Hunt in St. Paul's cathedral, a print of which hangs in her kitchen. It is remarkable that the door at which Christ stands and knocks has neither handle nor keyhole. The artist when asked to explain this omission had replied that it was the door of the heart that could only be opened from the inside.

Maybe she had been looking for the wrong sort of key all these years, the woman ponders.

She turns to her spinning wheel, always a means of bringing calm and comfort to her over active mind. The hands of the spinner hold many strands, plying the separate threads into one continuous and harmonious yarn.

This was what Susie was struggling to achieve at a time when there were so many demands coming to her from opposing directions and at different speeds. It was only the vision of the complete Rainbow Tree Exhibition which made it possible to weave all the new participants into the overall design. Although she had drawn a sketch of the 'New Rainbow Seeds', the structure of the patchworks had to be continually adapted to accommodate the children who would make them. This task was a much harder than any of the ballets she had choreographed, but the ability to see the entire finished work at the time of its conception was certainly an advantage.

Time to pause and to go back to the beginning of the Purple Seed.

Chapter Thirteen

THE PURPLE SEED

The Purple Seed was started, like the Rainbow Tree, in Iona. The first of the pair of patchworks was entitled 'The Elements'. The children (all eleven of them) in the tiny island school made the water section. After all they were completely surrounded by it so there was plenty of inspiration. Each hand painted strip showed a different aspect of this unpredictable and constantly changing substance. The young textile artists were surprised to find such variety in something they had always thought of as blue. Learning about colours was only one of the many new skills and talents that this innovate educational arts project was opening up. Awareness of their own and the other participants' environment was another important part of the seven-year venture.

The children in London, who would make the next two sections, already felt connected to their co-workers in Scotland and were eager to see what they had created when Susie returned. The fire section was a vibrant collage of yellows and reds decorated with sparkling sequins and flame-coloured braids, not to mention numerous beads and buttons bought in the multicultural markets on the Isle of Dogs.

The Bangladeshi children described the air in their inner city environment as black. They said it was 'full of fog and smoke and made them cough and choke' but some painted their strips a bright, clear blue saying that 'the air was cool and fresh in the mountains of Bangladesh'.

Susie invited one of the teachers from India to come to Britain to learn the process of making the new work. It was important that everyone followed the same principles and understood the overall concept linking the whole series although there was still considerable opportunity for individual creativity.

Mayaben arrived in early March and as it was her first visit to London, Susie allowed a few days to see the sights before they got to work. The first thing they did together was to attend evensong at St. Paul's cathedral. The historic building was within walking distance of Susie's flat and she often enjoyed the privilege of sitting in the ancient, carved choir stalls and listening to the sublime singing. Besides, it was the only way to get into the famous place of worship without paying. Both women were religious in their own ways and Susie had prayed with Mayaben many times in the little shrine in her home in India. This was integral to all Hindu households and as much part of daily life as cleaning, cooking and eating. It made no difference to either of them in what form or where the act of worship took place. After the service Susie showed her Indian friend the original painting of 'The Light of the World'. The beautiful symbolism made a deep impression on Mayaben and she was thrilled to receive a print like the one that hung in Susie's house.

The South Bank Centre was another favourite place in London. Susie had quickly discovered the many free amenities available in the richly endowed city and as one of the 'disadvantaged' (forced by circumstance to claim State benefit), she enjoyed reduced entry fees to many others. There was a jazz concert going on when they arrived at the riverside café. Abandoning all inhibitions the two women began to dance. People noticed the genuine joy as the unusual couple embraced on the ballroom floor, one in saffron sari, under a borrowed coat, upon which a shiny jet-black plait bounced. The other, in baggy Indian trousers and charity shop sweater, her short grey hair escaping from the bright yellow beret perched jauntily upon her head. They shared an invisible secret which both believed would grow into a whole forest of Rainbow trees before the second millennium ended.

The Indian teacher accompanied Susie and the spinning wheel to the Isle of Wight where the final corner of 'The Elements' was about to be made. The Middle School children were learning the ancient craft of spinning as part of the cultural background to the rural environment of the 'Earth' section. The fertile soil of this sheltered southern farming community lent itself to imaginative artistic images. Hand spun natural fibres gave added interest and dimension to richly coloured strips for earth is no more just brown than water is blue.

Now there was only the central seed shaped section to be completed. This was to be Mayaben's responsibility when she returned to India with the patchwork. She would lead the workshops at the children's Creativity Centre when they made the fifth element, known in their culture as 'Dharma', the divine spirit which links the other four together. The whole piece should be finished for the first Festival of Friendship to be held in India in October.

But first, a joint assembly at one of the London schools had been arranged to celebrate the Purple patchworks. It turned out to be a chaotic event with many crossed wires and tensions but it was the fact that children and adults from each group had made the journey to bring the separate pieces of work together that mattered. This was what united them when they were apart. This was what they all believed in and the wondrous results of their efforts surpassed every difficulty.

With 'The Elements' safely dispatched to India, Susie turned her attention to 'The Planets'. Work on this did not properly commence until after the Rainbow Tree's European tour, but at least the borders were underway by the time she returned in July. A new primary school on the Isle of Wight had recently joined the Rainbow Tree Project. The children were 'doing' the solar system and, as they knew far more about the planets than Susie, were delighted to take over the bulk of the new work. It was exciting to link education and textile art together. Both aspects took on added depths and meaning and inspired future collaborations.

By the middle of the autumn term the central section of 'The Planets' was complete and it only remained for Susie to whiz it up to

Iona so that the Scottish children could fill in the outer corners with 'unformed chaos'. Creative embroidery reached new heights of imagination with knots and tangles all part of the artistic effect. Commuting between Iona and the Isle of Wight was the easy part. Getting the giant Rainbow Tree and its purple seedling ready to take out to India was somewhat more challenging. Susie had two young volunteers from the Isle of Wight to accompany her this time, Tash, aged thirteen and Anna, aged twelve. The courage and trust of those two girls and their parents still seems astonishing...

There it is again. Trust.

* * *

The spinner in the sunny box contemplates the strength of the tiny frail fibres as they blend into a thread that becomes a yarn that becomes a chord. The triple chord of trust, commitment and belief can also be woven from the frailest of hopes. When two or three join their hopes together and act upon their beliefs miracles occur. When nothing is written, when no contract exists, when the only insurance is a promise, then trust goes hand in hand with the faith that moves mountains.

Susie believed that the Rainbow Tree would provide for all their needs. She told the children that unlike other trees it did grow money, but only when it was needed. The crock of gold that nestled under its roots conveniently bore fruit every Christmas and filled up Susie's travel fund just when it was nearly empty.

Eventually she plucked up courage, when her mother asked, 'Who's paying for all this?' to confess 'You are, Mum!'

At first it hadn't gone down too well and it was suggested that the annual cash gift should be put in a trust for Susie until she was older but when she reminded her mother that she would soon be an old age pensioner she agreed that it was probably too late for prudence or caution to prevail.

So it was that all the fares were provided until the last of the many journeys took the whole completed exhibition of fourteen patchworks to their final destination in Russia at Easter 2001.

But that is still far in the future in October 1995.

Tash and Anna spent several days staying in Susie's flat before setting off to India. London's multicultural East End was almost as different from the pleasant green island where the girls lived as the country they were about to visit. The preparations were an important part of the forthcoming trip and helped to allay any fear the young travellers may have felt. It was decided to take 'Ming', Susie's Chinese teddy bear, along with them. He had become a sort of mascot for the project and he still held many unspoken secrets entrusted to him long ago by the lonely little girl who was integral to the whole project. The two girls kitted 'Ming' up with a monsoon cloak made from an old umbrella, a pair of Bermuda shorts with matching T-shirt and a special blanket that Susie had knitted herself. The battered old bear even had his visa photograph taken and an emergency first aid kit, just in case.

At last the day of the flight came. Heavily laden with backpacks, handbags and overnight holdalls and the inevitable giant-sized laundry bag, the trio set off for Heathrow Airport via the London Underground. The air of excitement was heightened by the addition to the expedition of one of the Iona children. Joanna was only nine years old so her mother was accompanying her. They were flying straight down from Scotland and would meet Susie, Tash and Anna at the check-in desk.

The overnight flight went without a hitch, the three children glued, sleepless, to the film screen while the two women dozed uncomfortably curled up in their standard class seats. The plane arrived on time at Bombay airport. The travellers stood watching bag after bag swing round on the caravel, (one holding the precious Rainbow Tree in protective anonymity) waiting to be claimed by their owners. There was only one problem. Susie's much-travelled rucksack was missing. It contained only her few personal belongings but the loss had to be reported none the less. After signing a great many forms, answering endless questions and hanging about in hot stuffy offices, the bedraggled little party were eventually able to continue their journey to Ahmedabad.

When eventually the small local plane landed an hour and a half later, a traditional Indian welcome engulfed the startled travellers. Nothing Susie had said could have prepared them for the overwhelming excitement that greeted the weary group as soon as they set foot upon the sticky tarmac. Bouquets of wilting roses and gaudy carnations were thrust into already full hands, a sea of beaming brown faces and screaming shrill voices surged around the bewildered children before bundling them into various battered vehicles all waiting to rattle them to their final destination. They reached the first floor flat, borrowed for the three-week visit, just before midnight. Every effort had been painstakingly made to provide for the visitors' needs. Pritiben, the co-ordinator who had stayed in Susie's flat the previous year, had taken note of some eccentric Western requirements. Toilet paper, bottled water and Indian-style muesli were unusual luxuries to be found alongside packets of rice, lentils, fresh herbs, dried spices, wholemeal flour and curry sauce. The flat even had a bedroom as well as a living room so there was plenty of space to spread their exhausted bodies around. Space there was but peace there was not. Even in this comparatively quiet suburb, dogs barked, a late taxi hooted, radios blared and a quarrelling couple shouted through the dark, humid night. Peace, in India was an inner quality to be acquired at the earliest possible age as a matter of necessity.

* * *

Peace. The woman is surrounded by peace. The cottage garden lies in winter stillness. The trees are unruffled by rustling leaves, snow-sprinkled mountains sit like ancient Buddhas on the distant side of

Moray Firth, and the glass-cold sea shines silently beneath a brilliant, cloudless sky.

The woman is not at peace. She is disturbed by turbulent memories. She feels again the desperation that often drove her in those days when the bitter taste of bereavement haunted her. She could not escape from the pursuing sense of loss however far she ran away from the home and marriage she had left behind. The Purple Seed was not sweet and there were many difficulties to be surmounted that would have daunted her had not the work seemed so important. The Rainbow Tree and its seven seeds were the steps to healing but wholeness would not come until the end of the story.

* * *

A tremendous welcome awaited the Britishers the following morning. The dusty lanes of Juhapura village were lined with a singing, clapping crowd as two crammed rickshaw scooters deposited the group at the Creativity Centre. Around the entrance numerous brightly clad children, eager to touch the white skin of their special visitors, jostled for the best view before dragging them into the hall. 'The Elements' hung proudly upon the wall, complete with beautifully made central piece. An expectant empty space waited beside it. Anna and Tash duly unpacked 'The Planets' which took its rightful place and completed the Purple pair. This immediately inspired an outbreak of joyful celebrations sweeping away the last vestiges of fatigue from the jet-lagged travellers.

A few days later the main event of the 1995 Festival of Friendship took place in the centre of Ahmedabad. The whole town was invited, even compelled, to join in when the Rainbow Tree stopped the traffic. A group of fearless and deftly agile youths shinned up lampposts to sling the giant patchwork high above camel carts, reckless rickshaws, bumping bicycles and honking motorists. Even the policeman, standing on his central podium like a bandleader, was caught up in the

Carnival atmosphere and waved his arms about more in sympathy with the singing, dancing revellers than directing of the chaotic flow of traffic.

'Ming' became the unexpected star of a puppet show, brought along to amuse the excited children. He was awarded an Indian Princess's beaded headdress and a golden necklace for the performance but was much too polite to point out that he was the male descendant of a long line of distinguished Chinese philosophers.

Each day was crammed full of activities. Everyone wanted to see and talk to the young visitors from Britain. They were stoic in their attempts to cope with school visits, press conferences, teaching songs and dances to street children and participating in art and craft classes. It was hard, gruelling work with little time to acclimatise to the heat, the very different culture or the unaccustomed food. Each one of those three brave and plucky youngsters deserved a medal and gave Susie the hope and inspiration to carry on when her own energy threatened to desert her. The girls rose to the challenge of this intensive 'shared life experience' even when the toilet paper ran out and the water supply was limited to whatever they could carry up to the first floor flat from the communal pump in the yard below. Anna was particularly brave when she suffered a debilitating tummy upset and Tash became a kind and capable nurse to her friend, both youngsters finding qualities of inner strength that would help them in their future lives.

The last few days of that momentous trip in 1995 allowed time to enjoy a day out to a newly opened water park and a weekend in the country at Mr. Purwar's house, sleeping on the roof in the company of treetop monkeys and prowling peacocks. But the most popular activity was shopping. The local bizarre was packed with irresistible treasures of every conceivable sort, making shopping an experience way beyond their wildest dreams. This was retail therapy of the first order and never failed to bring excitement and wonder. Whole exhibitions took place with the dazzling contents of the extra suitcases, purchased in order to transport the treasures home.

The magic of India lived on in suburban sitting rooms and rural schools bringing warmth and colour into many a cold grey British day.

By the grace of God, the three girls and two women arrived safely home at Heathrow Airport to be met by relieved and grateful parents. The little party dispersed, anxious to complete their journeys to Scotland and the Isle of Wight as soon as possible. Susie returned home alone to her empty flat. The Rainbow Tree had a new bag, specially made and decorated with hand painted animals by an Indian craftsman. It seemed heavier than ever and the lost rucksack, though not retrieved until departure from Ahmedabad made an added burden. The borrowed clothes that she wore now, and throughout the trip, were as sufficient as the grace that had supplied all her needs.

Susie took a taxi home and fell into bed without bothering to take them off.

Chapter Fourteen

THE INDIGO SEED

News of the Rainbow tree was spreading. As soon as she returned from India, Susie was invited to fill the post of artist in residence at Beetham Primary School, Cumbria. She leapt at the opportunity to spend six months among the hills and countryside of the Lake District. It did not seem necessary to be based in London now that she was travelling so much. 'Home' seemed to have become her suitcase and she was reminded of the seven years touring with the Royal Ballet. Then, as now the focus was on what she was doing rather than on where she was living. But a longing for a real home was growing inside the traveller and she began to dream of that cottage in Scotland again. Cumbria was half way there and when the wind was blowing in a Northerly direction, she fancied she could smell the Scottish air.

She decided to put her London flat on the market and rent accommodation near the Cumbrian school. She didn't really intend to sell it, at least not for a while, but when an offer was made almost at once she couldn't resist it. It was a little less than she had paid for it but with extensive and expensive renovation pending it was a good time to get out. By the beginning of December 1995 Susie had moved and settled into a large bed sitting room with kitchenette and bathroom on the first floor of an old house in a small Cumbrian market town.

The children of Beetham Primary School made the first and central section of the new Indigo patchwork, 'Waterworks'. Their theme was the natural force of water and they created an image of a water wheel surrounded by symbols of how we harness this power. The top section, to be made in India, would show the sources of water and feature clouds, rain, springs and mountain streams. The bottom section, to be made in the Isle of Wight would focus on courses plotted across the sea. Whirlpools and dangerous currents took the form of monsters which the 'friend ships' had to be careful to avoid. The latter two thirds of 'Waterworks' could not be put into production until after Russia.

RUSSIA!

As planned, Susie went to Cheboksary, the capital of the Chuvashian Republic, at Christmas time. Yelena had kept her promise to arrange everything and the sister of another teacher, accompanied by a diminutive friend, met the Rainbow Tree co-ordinator at Moscow airport. The two Russians wasted no time in showing the visitor their famous city. 'Are you tired?' enquired the smaller woman.

'Not really,' replied Susie politely, meaning 'Yes'. She had yet to learn that 'yes ' means 'yes' and 'no' means 'no' in Russia.

'Then hurry please, we go to the circus.'

The tall and short women strode off at a great pace urging Susie to follow. The three of them struggled to cram her enormous suitcase into the boot of a waiting car. Something more weatherproof than the decorative Indian bag was needed to protect the ageing Rainbow Tree from the Russian winter. Gulia and Rita introduced themselves on the brief drive to the circus. As soon as they took their seats in the crowded tent, Susie was swept up in the spirit which had captivated her when she had experienced the thrilling passion of the Bolshoi Ballet's first visit to London in the 1950's. The flared nostrils of steaming, gleaming steeds bearing daring bare backed riders, the flamboyant antics of dazzlingly attired trapeze artists and the poignant humour of sad clowns swelled her heart to bursting. Caviar served on dry, black bread and washed down with cheap Russia champagne further contributed to Susie's ecstatic mood. Her emotions were all over the place. The lid had blown off years of suppression and sometimes she felt as turbulent as water in a storm-tossed sea. At others she would suddenly find herself plunged into a cold, loveless lake of desolation with the despair of the drowning swan queen but right now she was riding on a wave of exhilaration.

Next morning Gulia arrived promptly at the dingy door of the small flat Rita shared with her husband, his parents and her teenage son. Susie had been too tired the previous night to notice that she had been given the only proper bed and was deeply touched to discover that the family had made do with the sofa and floor for the sake of their guest's comfort. She hastened to get dressed for the day's outing to Red Square and the Kremlin.

The intense cold hit the three women as soon as they stepped out of the stuffy over heated apartment into the snow piled high at the entrance. Despite two pairs of gloves, a borrowed sheepskin coat and a fake fur hat Susie was nearly crying with cold by the time they reached St. Basil's Church. Oblivious of the fabulous interior of the unique building, she made straight for the first radiator in sight. The Russian women waited impatiently while she tried to defrost her frozen hands, advising the feeble visitor to wear more suitable clothes in future and urging her to admire the extraordinary architecture of the famous place. They could not afford to dally and there was much more to see before the afternoon train departed for Cheboksary.

The dazzling contents of the Kremlin museums have struck awe in many visitors to this bewildering country of contrasts but Susie was more impressed by what she saw outside. There was none of the downtrodden dreariness she had been led to expect. Instead there was a magical quality that seemed more alive than diamonds and rubies in a glass case. It seemed to shine like silver in the laughing eyes of red-cheeked children tobogganing down the steep slopes surrounding the fortress and to glow warmly upon the backs of new bronze statues of fairytale characters. The enthusiastic pride with which Rita and Gulia showed off their great city had the sparkle of emeralds and the dedication of the old women who polished brass handles and washed marble floors day after day reflected the endurance of gold.

There was barely time to squeeze in a visit to the nursery school of Gulia's two children and Susie was anxious about catching the four o'clock train. She was reluctant to unpack the Rainbow Tree from its carefully folded security in the new jumbo suitcase but the insistence of the teachers overrode her fears.

'We will do everything' they declared.

Rita said, 'trust me,' in the same confident manner with which Yelena had persuaded Susie to come to Russia, and promised to get her to the station on time.

The tiny children reacted in the way of all children when they saw the Tree of Friendship filling the small classroom. Language was not required to explain its message or to encourage them to add cut out images of their hands to the crowded international branches.

If it had not been for the unwieldy heaviness of Susie's luggage the journey to the station would have been made on the excellent metro system with its impressive mosaics, spacious platforms and incongruous chandeliers. As it was, Rita's husband collected the three women from the school in his jeep. He was nonchalant about the extensive traffic clogging Moscow's wide streets laughing at the visitor's constant glances at her watch. These Russians live recklessly, she thought, and appeared to have a much more relaxed attitude to time than was usual in Britain.

The train was revving up its engines when the breathless group hurried onto the platform. The Russians hastily escorted Susie to the sleeping compartment as she tried to explain about her need of assistance and lack of Russian to her three travelling companions. Gulia, Rita and her triumphant husband hugged their new friend energetically before jumping off the departing train and waving her farewell.

She settled down in the corner seat gazing through the grubby windows at the snowscape ceaselessly unfolding mile after mile. She pushed the hand embroidered linen curtains to one side to get a better view. It was a graceful scene. Slender silver birch trees rose as silently as dancers to populate the deserted countryside. She remembered how, as a child, she had enjoyed overnight journeys from Edinburgh to the Ballet school in Surrey. The fun of tucking herself up in a cosy little bunk and snuggling down to the comforting rhythm of wheels chugging through invisible miles was heightened when she woke up in a completely different place. Susie wondered what she would find when she arrived at Cheboksary next morning.

A loud knock interrupted her reverie. A fierce looking attendant, clad in official navy blue suit, slapped a large bundle, wrapped in a plastic bag, upon the seat.

Susie looked up enquiringly. Pointing to the upper bunk and miming sleep, the stern woman shrugged impatiently at the ignorance of the passenger. Her three companions, a young man and a middle-aged couple, came to her rescue ripping open the plastic container to reveal sheets, pillowcase, towel and face flannel. The sheets had been carefully mended in the 'sides-to-middle' fashion that was common in post war Britain. Once the sleeping bunk was properly made to the attendant's satisfaction, she rewarded the foreigner with a transforming smile and a tall mug of black tea complete with slice of lemon.

Susie slept well. It seemed a matter of minutes before she was awakened with another glass of hot tea. She dressed carefully and remembering how smart Yelena was, applied mascara and lipstick before adjusting the fake fur hat to best advantage.

The train slowed down as it approached Cheboksary giving Susie a chance to glimpse the large group of men, women and children waiting on the platform. A great welcome had been arranged to greet the first British visitor to the provincial city. Cameras flashed, voices rose and bouquets were held high from waving hands as Susie stepped out of the train. She felt like a star. The former ballerina was treated with the respect that all artists receive in Russia, even after retirement.

Yelena had written to Susie in London to ask how she was planning to introduce the Rainbow Tree project.

'What is your idea?' she had enquired, adding, 'you have no Russian.'

Good question, thought Susie when she had received the letter some months previously. Then it came to her. She would dance the story of the Rainbow Tree.

An assembly of head teachers had been arranged the day after Susie's arrival in Cheboksary. It was Monday morning. An air of anticipation trembled in the long, wide corridors of Lyceum No 1. Whispering children were waiting to be summoned to their seats. They were intensely curious to see the visitor of whom they had heard much from their teacher since her recent trip to Britain. When everyone was seated a hush fell upon the expectant audience.

Yelena switched on the cassette player as Susie had requested. The first deep, sombre chords of Gorecki's Polish lament seeped into the hall like morning mist. A masked figure stepped silently into the waiting space, her slight dancer's body disguised by the heavy robes she wore. A voice echoed between each resonating chord like a desert wind ruffling the sands of time. The voice soared on a wave of longing and the dancer lifted her arms throwing back her head in a soundless cry. Wave after wave of sound and movement swept in growing arcs, like unformed energy entering the void before the beginning of creation.

A different voice joined the singer. Spoken words came from within the mask.

'In the beginning there was only one seed.' The head of the dancer bowed down in the rough, ugly seed like shell in which it was enclosed. The lament gained momentum and the seed head suddenly broke open on a heartrending climax to reveal the face inside it.

The dancer spoke again, 'It was all alone in loneliness.' Her purple robe flew out in a swirling movement, throwing up her arms and propelling the broken seed into space.

'In it was all of life, crying out to be born.' The anguished voices of dancer and singer interwove in patterns around each other like shadows. Then in a frenzy of frustration the whirling figure ripped off her spangled robe as if to capture her invisible partner within it.

The music stopped. For a moment there was nothing but silence. Then creeping like water into rock pools when the tide turns, a softer note caressed the fallen dancer.

She slowly arose, wearing a new robe of darkest Indigo, lightened by flashes of brilliant turquoise as the flowing, unfolding drapes came alive with movement. The head inside the fragmented seed was now clad in a deep blue cap. Ribbons cascaded around the dancer's face like mermaid's locks. She seemed not to see the audience as she cradled the shell from which she had emerged with the embrace of a mother for her baby. Wrapping it in the Indigo robe, a simple pale blue tunic was revealed, its long skirt was as bright as a cloudless sky, its sleeves as sheer as air. Forgetting the pain of birth, forgetting the pain of living the dancer was lulled into a dream like state of deceptive peace.

Suddenly a storm erupted from nowhere. The dream became a nightmare and as the music became as wild as a hurricane the sleeping dancer was tossed about on waves of urgent sound. Her beautiful gown was torn from her body, the sparkling headdress thrown to the ground, leaving her stripped of colour, life and form. She sank to her knees and buried her bare head in her hands.

Then the music changed again and she opened her eyes to look around her. Four grey bundles lay like stones in front of the stage. She walked tentatively forwards and picking up the first one it fell apart exposing a grass green poncho inside its drab exterior. The dancer put it on and began to move like a plant pushing through the softening soil of spring. The music swelled. The plant grew into a tree swaying and bending and fluttering its leaves like the wings of a bird.

The next grey bundle contained a sun yellow poncho. The dancer draped it over the green. She seemed ageless as she assumed the freedom of wild animals, leaping with the grace of a gazelle and bounding in uninhibited exuberance.

The third poncho was orange, the colour of humanity. The dancer came back to herself and addressed the audience from her own heart. She told them that the final seed was full of hope. She invited one of the children to unwrap the remaining bundle and put on the red poncho as a symbol of the friendship she hoped they would enjoy together.

The applause assured Susie that the Russian teachers had accepted her and that the children would become the latest branch of the Rainbow Tree. They were eager to get started on the introductory project to make a small, collapsible Rainbow Tree for the school Christmas party. Susie had worked out the design before she left London and planned to use readily available and simple materials. The trunk was constructed from seven round cardboard boxes, in diminishing sizes, placed on top of each other in the style of Russian dolls, the branches made from tightly rolled and brightly coloured strips of newspaper with decorations consisting of all manner of ingenious and shiny objects.

Susie was swept up into school plays and endless repetitions of 'Jingle Bells', 'Rudolph the Red Nosed Reindeer' and 'White Christmas', dancing round the Rainbow Christmas Tree with class after class of children.

On Christmas Eve Yelena took her guest to the midnight mass in the blue and gold domed church in the old part of town. The two friends trudged through deep crunchy snow and into the heady atmosphere of beeswax candles, glittering icons and the poignant singing of a traditional Russian choir. It was a new experience for both of them. The Russian teacher had asked Susie to tell her pupils about the Christian Festival but no words could add to the sight and sound which embraced them now.

There was a brief holiday over New Year during which Susie was richly entertained in the small homes of several teachers with feasting on a grand scale. Roast goose, caviar, chocolate layer cake and champagne were a few examples of the rich fare produced out of tiny kitchens and consumed in crowded living rooms. Then table and chairs were pushed away to clear the floor for music and dancing. Nothing was spared to give the first British visitor to Cheboksary the best possible impression of the city. A car was borrowed for a sightseeing trip around the picturesque old town of domed church, wooden houses with intricately carved doors and window frames and wide walkways bordering the huge expanse of the river Volga. New factories, department stores and an enormous modern Opera house, all built of uniformly uninspiring concrete, were shown off with equal pride. The spirit of enterprise seemed undaunted by economic difficulties and despite the fact that the teachers were often unpaid and always poorly financially rewarded they put no less effort into the work they considered a vocation.

As soon as school reopened, the Rainbow Tree programme was planned to commence with the making the central panel of the second Indigo patchwork, 'Aquatic Life'. Then disaster struck.

A flu epidemic hit the town. The Ministry of Education ordered all schools in Cheboksary to be closed to avoid the spread of infection. The rest of Susie's visit would be wasted if there were no children with whom she could work. The head of Lyceum No.1 came up with an inspired idea inviting parents to allow their girls and boys to attend the workshops at their own risk. About twenty, aged between ten and thirteen, accepted. All lessons were cancelled giving an opportunity to concentrate solely the special project. Two art and craft teachers helped the children to make a stunning panel which would feature on the posters for the Millennium Exhibition of the completed Rainbow Tree series in the year two thousand. All the materials were bought in Cheboksary at the local haberdashery shop. Susie was surprised to find that she could get everything she needed as long as she knew precisely what that was. There was no baffling array of pre-selected goods on display as at home, instead the customer was required to state the exact amount, colour and size of each item before anything was produced from the glass case beneath the shop counter. Indecision and inaccuracy were not tolerated easily here.

The finished piece featured two giant fish, entwined in a 'yin-yang' embrace, and surrounded by a circle of brilliantly embroidered fish. More exotic aquatic creatures swam in an azure sea full of corals, seaweeds and feathery underwater plants. The result of the prolonged workshop was a bond of friendship and creative endeavour between Susie, the Russian children, their teachers and the unseen co-creators in Poland, India and Britain. When representatives from each of these groups came together at the 1996 festival in Cumbria they did not meet as strangers and plans to hold the 1997 festival in Cheboksary were already being laid before Susie returned home.

The success of the Russian trip was rapidly consumed in the hectic schedule of the remaining months of the Indigo Year. As well as regular trips to the Isle of Wight, where 'Waterworks' was being completed, another visit to India was arranged for March. Susie often felt more like an 'artist-in-travel' than in residence in the Cumbrian school, but the frequent train journeys provided opportunities to catch up on design work, sewing jobs and sleep.

This trip to Ahmedabad was to prove more demanding than the previous ones. Two mainstream schools had now joined the Rainbow Tree project and the educational aspect of 'Aquatic Life' required thorough preparation. The overall theme of water had very different implications in India than in the wet West coast of England or the seaside conditions of the Isle of Wight. The four corner sections, which were made in these different places, reflected the climate and environment of each. The Indian children had no problems in drying their hand painted pieces upon the scorching hot tiles outside the shaded classroom. The deep blues retained their intensity of colour in the quick drying heat and embroidering them could start without delay. In rainy Cumbria it took days for the dripping painted panels to dry, draped over radiators, and the children were dismayed to see that much of the colour was drained away. But Susie told them that this was an excellent example of experiential education and all part of the Rainbow Tree story.

With the patchwork pieces all well under way, Susie turned her attention to the forthcoming Indigo Festival to be held in June. As well as the group from Russia and the return of Pritiben, Vijay and Farzana from India, Yola had written from Poland to say that her school had raised funds to send her, three teenage boys and a male colleague to Cumbria for the three-week event.

Marvellous, thought Susie, but where was she to put them all? Perhaps it would be a good idea to move out of the rented accommodation and buy a property in the area with the proceeds from the London flat and a share of the recent sale of the former matrimonial home on the Isle of Wight.

Almost at once she came across a delightful barn conversion on one of her frequent country walks. The last unit was still for sale. It was a two and a half bed roomed cottage-style dwelling with modern interior, tiny fitted kitchen, wall to wall carpeting throughout and built in garage. As Susie did not own a car the latter would be ideal for an art studio and workshop area.

The purchase was completed a few weeks before the visitors would arrive for the Festival in June. Susie moved into her new home as quickly as possible. She augmented the furniture from her flat by buying twelve large foam rubber cushions, for sitting and sleeping upon, in preparation for the extended Rainbow Tree family.

They were all due to reach London on the same day but not at the same time or place.

Susie planned to meet each group herself and escort them to Cumbria by train.

The Indians were the first to arrive. The plane from Bombay touched down at Heathrow airport very early on the morning of June 22, 1996. It was a joyful and problem free reunion reminding the two women and two children of the original Rainbow Tree Festival in June 1994. They had all travelled a long way since then.

Susie still had friends in the block of flats where she used to live and had borrowed beds for her visitors to rest while she went to meet the next contingent.

The Polish group were due to arrive at Victoria Coach Station at midday having made the entire journey by bus. Yola, her colleague Pavel and the three boys were waiting in the arrival area when Susie hurried in breathlessly at five past twelve. Tomek, aged sixteen, his brothers Marchin, aged fourteen and Woyceck, aged twelve stretched out their hands as their teacher introduced them. They were pupils at the 'special needs' school where she taught. The boys' only special need was parents. As they had no one to go home to in the holidays they had been selected to come on the trip to Britain for the Festival of Friendship.

The Polish and Indian women had met in Iona two years ago when the giant patchwork tree hung on the walls of the abbey and Yola had first heard about the friendship project. They were delighted to see each other again and Susie left them and the youngsters happily eating and conversing together in all sorts of ingenious ways as she set off to collect the Russians.

Yelena's fax said that the flight arrived at 12 a.m. or was it 12 p.m.? Susie can't remember now but at the time she thought it meant midnight. The airport was completely deserted as she trudged wearily along the wide empty corridors that had seethed with passengers twelve hours ago. The silence was unnerving and she wondered where everyone was. Only a solitary cleaner, mournfully mopping mock marble floors shared the night with the lone woman.

'I've come to meet a flight from Russia,' she explained. Surveying the vast expanse of unmopped floor in front of him, the man fixed her with a despondent gaze.

'There won't be anyone here until the morning shift takes over at 3 o'clock,' he sighed. 'Oh dear,' Susie mumbled turning back towards the exit. She must have confused midnight with noon, she supposed, as she returned back from whence she came on the last tube of the night.

Twelve hours later she set out once more for London Airport. There was another unforeseen problem waiting to greet her at the tube station. London Underground workers were on strike and there were no trains to Heathrow that day. This meant taking a bus as far as possible and then completing the journey by taxi, an unwelcome expense. It was ten minutes past midday when Susie reached the arrivals lounge. Like the Poles, the Russians were waiting for the Rainbow Tree co-ordinator but as soon as Yelena, her nine year old daughter and another older girl and boy saw her all anxiety and frustration were wiped away with the tears of joy. On hearing about the tube strike, the Russian woman immediately asked, 'will the workers be punished?' Susie laughed at the idea and said that the return taxi trip would give an unexpected opportunity to see some of London's famous sights on their way to the railway station. She asked the driver to make a detour around Big Ben, the Houses of Parliament and Buckingham Palace, thinking that the problem might just as well be transformed into a bonus.

The arrangement was to meet the Polish and Indian groups at Euston Station. Both Pritiben and Yola were confident that they could make their own way there. That was before any of them knew about the strike. Buses were less reliable than the underground and Susie prayed they had decided to take a taxi instead.

Three hours and twenty minutes later the 4 o'clock train for Oxenholme-in-the-Lake District drew out of Euston station. Thirteen reserved seats remained empty. Five of the would-be occupants sat forlornly upon their suitcases at the platform entrance, the other eight were sitting in a stationary bus somewhere between Tower Hamlets and Euston Station. The divided party could do nothing but pray for the Rainbow Tree angel to reunite them and transport them to their joint destination.

Their prayers were answered and by midnight the eight youngsters and five assorted adults were safely tucked up in Susie's new Cumbrian home. The twelve foam rubber cushions made four beds upon the carpeted floors and the rest of the group filled the two and a half bedrooms.

The morning brought little encouragement to the inauspicious start to the 1996 Festival of Friendship. It was one of those wet days that was obviously going to last a week. A wet weather project was urgently required. This was where the built in garage came into its' own. Susie invited the boys and girls to decorate the bare brick walls in the style of their different countries. This would be an international art project and a permanent reminder of the unique gathering. The youngsters embraced the idea with enthusiasm and by the end of the week the garage was transformed, a mutual language been invented, friendships made and the sun had come out.

Beetham primary school's involvement in the Rainbow Tree had attracted a great deal of local interest resulting in invitations to visit three secondary schools in the Lake District towns of Coniston, Cartmel and Milnthorpe. They were keen to meet teachers and students from other countries and learn more about the educational art project.

The Indian, Polish and Russian groups made a great impression wherever they went. Displays of national dancing and dramatic presentations of the different cultures were very popular. The completed Indigo hangings, 'Waterworks' and 'Aquatic Life' were also widely admired and all three of the secondary schools wanted to participate in the next stage of the Rainbow Tree textiles. Susie's work in Cumbria was expanding. The six-month residency had come to an end and there was no further funding available but she agreed to continue in all four schools on a voluntary basis. Members of the art staff were enthusiastic and cunningly managed to combine the themes of the Blue, Green, Yellow and Orange years with the national curriculum. This connection was to prove as important and long lasting as the Russian one.

Susie's barn conversion buzzed with activity every evening. A cloth was laid out on the floor for the daily feast. The adaptable cushions made a circle around a central candle and grace was sung in the universal words that everyone understood. Food and laughter united hungry hearts as well as stomachs and individual identities were forgotten in the bosom of the Rainbow Tree family.

The final part of the festival took place in London at St James Church, Piccadilly. Although Susie was no longer a regular member the rector still welcomed her whenever she was in town and had invited the foreign visitors to participate in the Sunday service. The congregation was used to Rainbow Tree and other events and were not surprised to see a huge parachute of dark blue material, shining with sequined stars, spread out in front of the altar when they entered the church.

The story of the Lonely Seed had reached a new chapter. It was no longer lost in Purple space but travelling through Indigo water. The two new patchworks hung over the balconies on either side of the raised marble platform upon which the drama began to unfold.

Susie stood alone in the centre holding up a tiny fragment of the original seed in cupped hands. Eight young heads protruded from prostrate bodies hidden under the midnight blue parachute. The boys and girls imagined they were invisible and it was not until Susie whispered each of their names that they rose silently from the sleeping sky.

'Tomek', the voice called softly, 'Anna, Vijay, Woyceck,' it went on. Each figure responded like a sleep walker until Misha, Natasha, Marchin and finally Farzana joined the circle of dancers. Their cloaks swirled like clouds in a cold grey dawn and then whirled with the force of thunder and lightening when a storm erupted over the unborn earth. The dancing fabrics absorbed their fear of exposure and dissolved all differences of age, sex, nationality and ability. The drama ended with the tranquillity which follows a hurricane and the turbulent waters stilled into a calm peace. The Indigo year handed on the process of creation to the cool pale blue of air.

At the end of the church service the rector invited the visitors to introduce themselves by telling the congregation their names and country of origin.

'Vijay from India, Natasha from Russia, Marchin from Poland,' the confident voices rang out until they reached the end of the row. The last boy stood up and turning to face the assembled company with a broad smile lighting up his face, he declared,

'I am Misha from India.' A startled pause rippled along the pew. Then the Russian boy let out a great laugh. 'Oh! I forgot,' he said, 'I am from Chuvashia.'

Everyone knew he had said it all.

Chapter Fifteen

THE BLUE SEED

Air. Free as air, the air we breathe, the air which moves around us and, if we are a flock of birds, the air we travel through, rest upon and ride with. These were the topics of the pale blue year in 1996-97.

But something else is happening in the sunny box. The rhythm is changing. The currents sweep and swirl and sometimes sing around the seated woman enticing her into the cool, blue space outside.

Yesterday, when she was out walking, she found a lovely place within herself. A place where she can keep her own self company. She is stepping out, not of herself but with herself into air that is so fresh and clear and thin that it is like drinking champagne. The feeling of intoxication is one that began during the two years spent in the Lake District.

* * *

Whenever Susie walked on top of the immense hills and drank in the peace of the lakes she experienced an intoxicating sensation of flying. The first time it happened was the day she walked up to the top of Helvellyn in her Polish sandals.

It was a glorious day in October. The schools were on holiday and she was free to take advantage of a 'Pensioner's Day Rover' bus ticket. This allowed the passenger to hop on and off as many buses and take as many journeys as she wished between 10 o'clock in the morning and 9 o'clock at night. She had no intention of staying out that long but was eager to explore the famous walking areas. Susie put a couple of tangerines in one pocket and a few sweeties in the other and set off to catch the bus to the North lakes. She climbed to the top of the double-decker and settled into her favourite seat at the very front.

'Where to, Miss?' the conductor enquired.

'Just put me off somewhere nice for a long walk,' Susie replied with what she hoped was a winning smile. She was in a holiday mood and was determined to make the most of the fine weather.

'Helvellyn's nice,' said the young man with a cheeky grin. Susie didn't notice the tongue in his cheek but later she supposed he thought she was a tourist going off to climb a mountain in her sandals.

That was exactly what she did!

The few people she met on the increasingly steep footpath gave her funny looks when she asked if it was much further to Helvellyn. The picture of a cosy teashop with scones and cream began to fade as the terrain roughened and the climb toughened. But Susie kept going revelling in the space, the air and the glory of it all. She imagined spending many more days like this when the Rainbow tree project was completed and she could retire.

When Susie reached the top of the mountain path a breathtaking panorama spread out before her. She discovered later that it is called 'Striding Edge'. She strode. Stretching out her ballet dancer's legs, the woman rejoiced in her body. It had been restored to a new life and now her soul and her body danced together. No longer were they separated as they had been at the beginning of the journey of transformation over ten years ago. To have reached this high plateau, without the aid of the stick upon which she used to rely, and with only light sandals upon her feet, seemed like a miracle.

Six hours later, Susie came down to earth in a place called Ambleside. The last bus had gone and there was no hope of getting home that night. She found a guesthouse where she could have bed and breakfast, a hot bath and an excellent supper of fish and chips with a pint of beer. Then she slept. For ten dreamless hours she slept. The former dancer did not think that she had slept so well since the days when she would collapse, spent and satisfied, after performing a three-act ballet. As then, she awoke refreshed and restored with new energy.

Immediately after a hearty breakfast, the enthusiastic walker bought a pair of boots and set off again. Susie walked for three days. On the last she finally caught up with the bus and was a little disappointed that the cheeky young conductor was not on board to share her triumph.

The holiday over, it was time to get to work on the blue patchworks. The first one, 'Wind, Clouds and Sky', was started in Chebosary on Susie's next visit. The glorious autumn weather extended to Russia and she enjoyed two days of sunshine and walking in the palace parks of Moscow before the school term began. Children wore golden halos made from plaited beech leaves and danced round the resplendent trees while whole families gathered for huge and elaborate picnics.

As soon as Susie arrived in Cheboksary work began on two side panels depicting puffy clouds and rain-streaked skies. These would surround a central triangular section to be made later by 'O' level art students of Dallam School, Cumbria. They produced a striking design entirely out of their own imagination. The silk painting showed a dramatic bird-like creature with elaborate American-Indian headdress. Bright pinks, lilacs and blues embellished the face in spiralling and intricate patterns and a pair of huge eyes stared above a fiercely blowing mouth.

The Russian children in another Chuvashian school, embroidered a circle of migratory birds to fly around the centre section of 'Birds of Travel' when it was made in India in the following March. The journeys made by the winged creatures formed interesting geographical links between the different countries involved in the Rainbow Tree project.

When Susie returned to Cumbria she concentrated on the final section of 'Wind, Clouds and Sky'. This was painted and embroidered by teenagers at John Ruskin School in Coniston. Their piece captured the spirit of the sky which, in this part of the country, is often indistinguishable from the clouded hills and reflective water below. When it was combined with the bold 'Face of the Wind', the movement of the Russian side panels and a pale blue border, full of air borne objects, the overall effect was a complimentary and cohesive whole.

Susie had a travelling companion for the 1997 trip to India. Sharon had just left Dallam School and was looking for opportunities to explore the world before going to university. When someone introduced her to Susie they hit it off straight away. The teenager was relieved to find an old age pensioner so unstuck in her ways and the older woman was impressed with the maturity of the school leaver. More importantly, they shared a sense of humour that would stand them in good stead during future difficulties. Two prime examples were when Susie had all her traveller's cheques stolen and another time when they flooded Pritiben's flat in Ahmedabad.

The trip revolved around the second blue work, 'Birds of Travel', but it also provided ideal opportunities for Sharon to acquire experience in schools of another culture before embarking on a teacher's training course at the end of the year.

The three groups of Indian children were from very different educational institutions. An academic, English speaking school focused on migratory patterns and air pollution and made an additional hanging called 'The Air We Breathe' while the original Creativity Centre would concentrate on the borders for 'Birds of Travel'. The third group were in a special school based on the philosophy and beliefs of Gandhi. They made a central panel that was as striking and original as 'Face of the Wind'. The design by five boys, chosen by their class mates, showed a large seed shape in which two swans were entwined. The graceful, white birds had a special significance in Hindu mythology, the boys explained, the flared, cupped wings forming the carriage for the Goddess of Wisdom and Knowledge. These beautiful creatures are thought to be wise enough to distinguish between milk and water and if given a mixture of both to drink will extract only the former. The swans were surrounded by the circle of lesser birds of travel sewn onto a silk strip in Russia and now brought to India via Cumbria.

A new school on the Isle of Wight had made the outer corners for 'Birds' in the first couple of months in 1997. Second year primary children, as young as six, were studying weather patterns in the set curriculum. Susie and their imaginative teacher showed the children how to trace weather maps from newspapers and pin them onto silk strips. They then sewed over the pencil marks with running stitch with remarkable skill and concentration in such young children. Slightly older children from a neighbouring school, made individual felt birds and attached them to the 'sky' with tiny pieces of velcro. These birds really could migrate from place to place and often 'flew' to the other side of the patchwork and landed on a different piece of sky all-together.

All the separate strips had been transported to India and Sharon and Susie spent many hours in the little Indian flat, sprawled out on the cool marble floor, sewing all the pieces together with yards and yards of pale blue satin ribbon. This and most of the other trimmings and materials were bought in one of the famous markets in Ahmedabad, the heart of the Indian textile industry. The whole patchwork was completed with a border of assorted flying creatures made by children from the original Creativity Centre. Vijay was now too grown up, at the age of fourteen to attend the after school activities but often came to help Susie and Sharon with the sewing and made his own special contribution to the piece.

When 'Birds of Travel' was finished it was an exceptional piece of textile art and was proudly displayed for all the parents to see. Susie and Pritiben took the opportunity to explain the philosophy and aims of the Rainbow Tree project and the forthcoming Festival of Friendship in Russia in May. To their amazement several parents expressed a desire for their children to participate, even to the extent of paying their airfares themselves. Indians going to Russia was beyond even Susie's wildest dreams. It was a great affirmation of her work and the trust that Pritiben had devotedly built up over the past year. To arrange this barrier-breaking venture would require more tenacity and perseverance than ever but both women were determined to try to make it happen.

When Susie got home from India there was much to organise before the Russian trip. As well as the Indian group, Sharon and three twelve year olds from Beetham School, Cumbria were to come to the Spring Festival in Cheboksary. A preparation programme was arranged to acclimatise the girls with the different life-style, food and accommodation they were likely to encounter in a country that could not offer the daily luxuries that are taken for granted in Britain. Susie held Russian weekends in her cottage and invited the girls to come and stay. They enjoyed sharing a room and learning a few simple Russian words but were not so keen on the beetroot soup! More practical matters, like obtaining visas, booking flights, organising the programme over long distance telephone calls to Yelena, sewing loops onto the patchworks and preparing next year's designs were piling up on Susie.

There were problems in India too. Pritiben had left her post as co-ordinator for the Creativity Centre for another job so was unable to accompany the group of children to Russia. Someone else would have to be found.

The weight of the project seemed to be getting heavier and the full load still rested upon Susie's aching shoulders alone. She was also worried about money. She took advice from her mother's solicitor. He suggested that a separation settlement could be drawn up between Susie and her estranged husband to provide some security for her advancing years without the finality of divorce. This did not seem necessary, as although both of them had formed new friendships, neither had expressed any desire to re-marry since December 1992.

At that time, Susie had spent a post Christmas retreat in India at the

Benedictine Abbey near Bangalore. She was still deeply troubled about the break up of her marriage and had prayed for forgiveness and healing of the painful rift between her husband and herself. She even hoped that 'in time, we could come together in the accepting friendship and loving peace my parents experienced in the last decade of their marriage.'

But on returning to London there was a letter waiting for her from her husband telling her that he had fallen in love and wanted to marry again. He wanted her to be the first to know and he hoped she could share in his new happiness. She did try, even to the extent of going to the Isle of Wight to meet the lady and offering to give her husband an amicable divorce. However, the love affair did not last and the plans came to nothing. Now, four and a half years later, a little yellow hope sprang up again, like a spring crocus, as she went to put the proposal to her husband. Susie laid the separation agreement out on the walnut coffee table bridging the cold distance between them. Her husband studied the words in silence. It was an unpretentious proposal for a small lump sum and a modest annual income to augment her pension. He agreed on condition that the latter would be forfeited if she re-married. Susie immediately said she would never get married again.

'But I might.' he said.

This unexpected remark threw her completely off balance. The yellow crocus bent its head to the ground as his words sank into her comprehension.

'And,' he concluded, 'I would want to look after her.'

Hope died. She had never felt so alone. No amount of money could compensate for the desolation she felt on returning to the cold Cumbrian cottage. The wet, windswept fields outside were filled with furrows of liquid mud and a bleak, grey wind seemed to seep through the walls and under the new front door. A deep depression wrapped its heavy, black cloak around her. She couldn't cope, it was all too much, there was no one to turn to, she had lost her way. Susie crept into bed, drew the curtains, pulled the duvet over her head and fell into a deep sleep.

THE DREAM BEGINS

She dreamt that she was falling into a silver pool of sparkling water seemingly suspended between two mountains. It was shaped like a spoon and she could see a face reflected in the mirror-like surface. A spoon face. It was the face of a child and the child was dying, but she was not sad, she was singing. The lovely music behind the singing enfolded the child with all the tenderness of love. Susie dreamt she was falling in love. Love picked her up and swept her away in his arms before she fell into the icy cold water. Her prince had come at last. He promised to look after her forever more; he said he wanted to spend the rest of his life with her.

Susie said, 'I want to marry you.'

They stood by the silver pool and Susie saw a tree growing beside its lapping edge. The tree had grown into one circular branch like an unbroken ring of shiny golden wood framing the face of the prince. He was tall and handsome, his eyes lit up with love for her, he looked long and deep into her trusting gaze. She put her head through the golden ring beside the silver spoon pool and kissed him. Then they ran away hand in hand leaving everything they feared behind them.

A storm gathered in great dark clouds of screaming birds. Voices screaming in pain and blame swooped around the runaway lovers. They ran and they ran until they came across a tiny white church in the middle of a field. It was snowing and it was dark. It was the darkest day of the year; the day of the winter solstice; the day before the light returned to the Northern Hemisphere. Susie and her Prince dived into the little white church and slammed the door shut. They locked out the black birds of fear and the voices they could no longer hear.

There was to be a wedding in the church. A woman with a soft voice and wispy hair told them so. She was arranging white roses and yellow crocuses and golden branches of a broken tree upon the windowsills. There were big creamy candles upon the piano and a lace tablecloth upon a table set in the centre of the church.

'The minister is coming,' said the wispy woman. 'He is coming to marry you.'

She gave Susie a white blouse to cover her wet clothes and the Prince re-robed himself with effortless grace into a wedding suit of finest silk. The minister wore the kilt and his voice boomed out with the same resonance as the Scottish minister who had made such a wonderful speech at her first wedding.

It dawned on Susie that she and her Prince had run all the way to Scotland. She had come home; she was deliriously happy and madly in love.

They moved into a beautiful house on top of a hill. Its huge windows looked out to the snow-capped mountains and there was a spring in the garden that gave them fresh, clear water to drink. The sun shone continuously and so brightly that they had to wear sunglasses in bed. The light shone relentlessly into the darkness of night giving them no peace. Susie began to long to creep back into the darkness, into oblivion, into sleep. Even happiness was more than she could bear.

The prince was often silent and sullen for days on end and his eyes bored holes in her heart and cast shadows of doubt in her mind. Perhaps he did not really love her after all? She felt straggling threads of doubt wrapping around her. She tried to pluck them away but they clung to her feet and entangled her legs dragging her backwards until she was forced to turn around and look back. The threads were coming out of her own body. It was disintegrating, unravelling like an old piece of knitting as if her whole life was being ripped up into a shapeless and meaningless tangle.

* * *

Susie woke to find the old sweater, she had been too tired to take off, entangled about her feet. She must have tossed and turned all night for it to have travelled from the top of her body to the bottom and was even more unravelled around the hem than before. It was only fit for the scrap box now. The children would enjoy unravelling the wool and no doubt could use it in the new 'Green and Growing' patchwork.

Susie lay back on the crumpled pillow, the very thought of the next year's work making her feel exhausted.

She had recently returned from Russia. The Festival had been a great success. The two pale blue patchworks surpassed all previous efforts and expectations for the Green year were great. But her mind was as depleted of ideas as her body of energy and her spirit flagged wearily behind both.

The Russians had put on a terrific show in impressive style and she felt a comforting glow remembering the huge performance in the Children's Palace of Creativity.

Five hundred young dancers, singers and actors had taken part in the celebrations including the four Cumbrian girls who had accompanied Susie to Cheboksary. Sharon and three twelve year olds had choreographed their own original Morris dance and won the hearts of the audience in garlanded straw hats and little red shoes. Susie was proud of them.

It had not always been easy but the preparation programme helped to smooth the rough bits. One girl was a vegetarian, something that the Russians found difficult to understand and a 'luxury' in which they could not afford to indulge. Meat was an essential ingredient in the daily diet of most people and in such a cold climate it was probably a necessity. Perhaps, it was just as well the Indians had not been able to come in the end as Hindu Vegans would definitely have had problems sitting next to someone chewing a chicken leg. It had been a devastating disappointment when, at the last minute, a particularly stubborn immigration officer had refused to grant visas for the group from Ahmedabad to travel to Russia but on reflection, Susie felt it might have been a blessing in disguise.

As it turned out, the Indian branch had already made its final contribution to the Rainbow Tree project. Without her close friend and colleague to co-ordinate the work, to which both Susie and Pritiben had dedicated so much, it would not be possible to carry on. But they had achieved more than either had anticipated. The beautiful creations of so many children bore testimony to the belief that became the motto of the Rainbow Tree project.

'May the work of our hands, express the hopes of our hearts,
Reaching out to touch yours now.'

Chapter Sixteen

THE GREEN SEED

By the end of 1997 Susie was in real danger of burn-out. She desperately needed help if the project was to be completed. There were still three years to go until the millennium when the Rainbow Tree would drop its final seed onto the earth. That would be the Red Seed of Hope but it seemed a very long way off at the beginning of the Green Year. Yet another secondary school had joined the Cumbrian group and now that the Indian branch had dropped out, the two main groups were in Russia and the Lake District of England. Even the loyal primary schools on the Isle of Wight were struggling to find time to devote to the Rainbow Tree project in a national curriculum that squeezed creativity into tighter boxes and limited handcraft to a few short modules in the Design and Technology slot. Susie's suggestion that the two remaining schools made their own contributions in their own time, instead of being constrained to the format of the main designs, was welcomed.

She was therefore able to simplify the Green patchworks drastically and reduce her travel schedule considerably. She decided that she really needed a complete rest from overseas' trips. Four teachers from the Cumbrian schools volunteered to go to Russia in her place the following Easter when the textile sections would be ready to be assembled together. Susie's imagination failed to produce anything more interesting than four squares, each approximately one metre in size, for 'Green and Growing'. She left the design and contents entirely up to the art teachers and students in the two Russian and two English schools to whom she distributed the bare pieces of calico. A large border was added on order to accommodate the growing number of children, in both countries, who wanted to contribute to the textile exhibition. This had forty eight individual small squares of cotton that could be decorated with symbols of plant life and soil formations. These proved very popular with younger children and enchanting miniatures of beetle tea parties, earwig fashion models, sprouting beans and daisy chains were examples of how a tiny piece of simple fabric can become a work of art.

The second patchwork was even simpler. It consisted of one main piece designed and made by Shoumerlya Gymnasium in the rural regions of the Chuvashian Republic. News of the innovative educational textile art project was travelling fast in Russia. Schools there seemed to have more freedom than in the present technology-obsessed climate in Britain to develop extra curricular initiatives. 'Our Shared Earth' was meant to be shared by one of the Cumbrian Schools but Susie was informed that as it was to become 'a centre of excellence', concentrating on modern languages (including Russian), there was no longer time for hand-craft. That to link with real, live Russian youngsters in a creative way might offer the chance to converse together about a shared piece of work, escaped the notice of the English School. This seemed to Susie a sad example of a lost opportunity and added to her growing feeling of disillusionment.

A retired teacher offered to help co-ordinate the Rainbow Tree project in Cumbria but after six months hard work (funded by Susie) she was unable to continue. None of the participating schools were able to contribute to the considerable expenses incurred for materials, postage and printing etc. and even the request for a modest subscription of ten pounds a term was beyond the school budgets. These were hard times indeed.

The Lake District didn't seem such a good place to be after all. What would she do when the project was finally finished? The future loomed gloomily ahead in a frightening void. Susie crept back into bed and began to dream again.

THE DREAM CONTINUES

It was snowing. Huge drifts obscured the view from the picture windows and shut out the light. She struggled to push the back door open but although it creaked and groaned it would not budge. She was imprisoned in the house with the Prince. He was still sleeping, He seemed to sleep most of the time now and often did not speak for days. Susie was bored and lonely. She wanted someone to play with.

Someone came. He came all the way from India to play with her. It was the boy with the flute. He could make walls disappear and doors invisible when he played his flute. Susie remembered how they had danced through shop windows, held hands under London Bridge and floated above tall concrete blocks on the wings of the magic music at the First Festival of Friendship. The Indian boy opened the door for her and they both ran over the white hills so lightly that they left no footsteps. Their laughter echoed in the deep black valley between the sparkling hills and gathered a thousand children's voices into a deafening cascade that hurtled back to wake the sleeping Prince. He roared like an ogre. Fear clutched at Susie's heart.

The boy turned to look into her frozen eyes. He held out his flute to her and said, 'Take this and do not be afraid, for I am always with you.' The flute had turned into a silver cross. 'Go back to your husband and give him this.'

Her playmate vanished. Susie walked slowly and calmly back to the house. She walked through the open door and straight up the stairs to where her husband lay. She laid the silver cross upon the bed and said, 'I am going now, I do not need a husband anymore.'

He roared and shook his fist but Susie took no notice and quietly left the room.

The snow had gone. Everywhere was green and growing. Susie too was growing. She was as tall as the silver birch tree and her hair turned golden in the sun. Her legs were so long that she stepped over a wide, rushing river with one graceful movement and her arms reached up to the clouds. Her feet were huge. They made great hollow footsteps wherever she trod which immediately filled with yellow crocuses. The earth was brimming over with fertility. Flowers sprang into being all around her and a forest of slender, swaying trees fluttered their leaves against her face.

A narrow path cut a straight ribbon of light between the shadow-dappled trunks. On and on the woman strode, like a giantess making her fearless way. Nothing could frighten her now. She had grown up at last.

Suddenly a voice pierced the heart of the giantess. She fell to the ground as if shot by an arrow. The voice of a child shouting and crying bitterly hit the huge woman in her ears. Cowering down, afraid of the screaming child, the giantess shrank. She could not move; she could not get up; she sank into the mud.

'You can't forget me,' cried the little girl. 'I can leave you but you can never leave me.'

'Don't leave me here on my own,' the tiny woman wept, tears streaming down her shrivelled face. She was old now, a little old lady with no one to look after her.

'You can't expect me to look after you,' the child had become an angry young woman.

'You must clear up your own mess, look what a mess you have made!'

The young woman turned her back on the pathetic old lady and picked her way deftly and daintily through the undergrowth. Her pointed toes were encased in shiny, pink satin ballet shoes and she wore a crown on top of her neat, tight hair.

Susie did not give the snivelling old witch another look. The witch was the mother of the Prince and had no power over the ballet dancer who had escaped from both of them. She leapt and skipped through the dark green forest, jumping over sodden bracken, her shining feet soared high above the muddy puddles on either side of the ribbon path of light. It began to flow underneath her like a river and carried her upon white feathery waves until it ran into a silver pool of sparkling water.

Looking around her she saw a tree growing beside its lapping edge. A *broken ring of shiny, golden wood lay beneath its shattered trunk on the very spot where, once upon a time, she had kissed a prince. She bent down to stroke the fragments of her dream and there, sitting by the water's edge, was a large frog.*

'I'm not going to kiss you,' Susie laughed scornfully. 'You might turn into a prince.'

With that parting quip she leapt onto the snowy white back of a passing swan which swept her away with breathtaking speed. The great bird sped like lightening to the far end of the pool, spreading out like a vast lake, under its billowing wings. The swan stretched its long, thin neck forward unfolding its wide wings and flapping them with loud moaning sounds that echoed up from the vanishing ground.

Susie looked down and saw the witch waving an ancient broomstick at her and the frog sitting on her hunched back pretending to be a cat. They could not catch her now. She was free.

The swan flew higher and higher until they were far above clouds resembling the vast snow deserts in Russia. She clung onto the warm neck of the travelling bird wondering if it was migrating towards the eastern sun or flying back to the Northern light. The air got colder and colder, her bare shoulders froze in the icy wind and her arms grew numb. She felt herself slipping from the swan's back, falling down and through the non-existent clouds.

It was springtime when Susie woke up. There was still a chill about the bright mornings. She pulled the duvet around her bare shoulders with her right arm. The left one was quite numb. She must have been sleeping on it the wrong way. Rubbing it thoughtfully, she wondered what to wear. The barn conversion-cottage was draughty, having high ceilings and open plan rooms to give the illusion of the space it lacked. She decided not to 'cast a clout until May was out' and pulled on a thermal vest under a yellow silk shirt and the green cotton sweater she had inherited from her brother's wife. Jane had died of cancer but the radiance of her last weeks on earth still gave strength and hope. She needed both now. It was the first day of the school term and she was expected at morning assembly.

The four teachers, who had recently been to Russia at Easter 1998, had brought back many memories of the Green Year Festival. They had been suitably impressed with the skill and enthusiasm of the young performers who celebrated the completed patchworks with customary aplomb. They had also brought back gifts and souvenirs, countless letters from eager would-be pen pals and picture books of the beautiful Chuvashian countryside presented as gifts from the Minister of Service and Tourism. There had not been room in their luggage to bring back the two bulky patchworks from Russia. They would have to be collected by Susie next year.

'Our Shared Earth' still lacked a border. It was noticeable from the photographs that the large central seed-shape was crying out to be surrounded by a wealth of new growth to compliment and balance the 'Green and Growing' border. Susie did not know that in 1999 a group of Scottish children in Elgin would solve this problem. Right now, it was one of many things that she did not want to think about.

The day had exhausted her. She needed to rest but her restless soul would not lie down. It took flight like a seed on the back of the wind soaring high above the mist shrouding Susie's sleeping body.

THE DREAM ENDS

She was flying again. It was a glorious feeling, light as air, as simple as swimming. It was like light breathing. She felt as spacious as grace, free and graceful as space without form. She was free from thought, free from planning, free as air.

Life was rising, breathing, beating all around her like the wings of unseen birds, but inside she was still. Still and spacious, simply gracious, letting Life live her.

Effortlessly, she glided down to earth and landed silently upon a wide, deserted beach. There was not a soul to be seen, not a sound to be heard except the gentle sigh of transparent ripples of unfurling water upon the pale, golden sand. She walked along the edge of the pale, golden sand and dipped her bare feet into the clear water. Like stroking hands, the rhythm of the soft curls of seawater caressed her pointed toes.

A pink house suddenly appeared on the corner of the bay. It had a beautiful garden leading down to the beach. The gate was wide open. Walking up the path she saw that the door to the house was also open. A sound like singing could be heard but no human voice could be so clear and soft and pure. She followed the sound and entered the house until she found an angel playing a harp. Had she been sitting on a cloud she might have been in heaven, but the angel had her feet firmly on the ground.

'Do you do bed and breakfast?' enquired Susie. She was looking for a place, a space where quiet waters flow and she could lie low for a while.

'Of course,' replied the angel, laying her harp carefully upon the polished wooden floor. 'How long would you like to stay?'

'Until I have found my home,' Susie found herself saying.

'I know of a small, stone cottage upon a sweet hillock, not far from here.'

The angel took Susie by the hand and led her to the open window pointing up to the distant hills beyond a forest of fir trees.

'See,' she said, 'this is your home. It has been waiting for you to come for a very long time.'

She placed a small key in Susie's hand and said, 'go now, go and unlock the light that is within you and you will never be lonely again.'

The angel went on, 'the house of the Lord is your dwelling place. I have prepared it myself, it is ready for you now.'

Susie was not sure if she understood exactly what the angel was telling her, but she followed her directions and saw a narrow road turning off to the right just beyond a small railway bridge. Sure enough, there was a row of three stone cottages each with a little garden in front of them exactly as the angel had said. The end cottage had a glass box, full of light, attached to the back door.

Susie's guide had told her that this was the way in. There was no lock on the door, not even a handle. Gently pushing it open she suddenly felt a rush of energy ignite within her. It was as if a flame had been lit in her heart. She looked down at the small key she still held in her hand. It sparkled like gold, it flickered like fire, it fluttered like a butterfly and rose into the air with the silent grace of a bird. The key flew out of the open door and disappeared from sight.

Susie stood quite still and watched it go. She began to understand something she had heard a very long time ago. The key to God's house was indeed a little light inside her. She had found what she had been looking for since she was seven years old.

Chapter Seventeen

THE YELLOW SEED

The woman sits in the sunny box. It is full of light and a white frost decorates the grass like icing on a cake. Now, in her fourth spring here, the cottage on the sweet hill feels like home. It is a relief to be able to sit in one place for as long as she likes.

Wriggling her feet inside the fur-lined slippers, a present from Russia, her toes, she imagines, feel like the tender roots of new growth reaching down into their native soil. She often thinks of herself as a plant. When she first started coming back to Scotland from the damp, mild South, she described her marked improvement in health by saying, 'I just seem to grow better here'.

It was as if she had been transplanted back into the climatic and environmental conditions in which she could thrive.

* * *

Susie certainly felt like that in the summer of 1998. It was on holiday in Morayshire, following a visit to her mother in Crieff, that the determination to move back to Scotland took root in her mind. She had not settled in Cumbria and wanted to move again. The barn conversion was what the estate agent called 'a desirable property' and should not be difficult to sell. She put in on the market and rented a cottage in the heart of the Highlands, gambling that she would sell and re-buy by the end of six months.

The Yellow Year's topic of 'Wilderness' seemed appropriate during all the wandering steps that eventually led Susie to her final home. She was still lacking in inspiration for the textile art project and the designs for the two new patchworks were as simple as the previous year. This time she divided the two-metre squares into triangles; four squat ones for 'Mountains and Deserts' and four elongated ones for 'Wild Animals'. The making of the patchworks was shared by the schools in Russia and Cumbria and the Swedish pen friends of Beetham Primary School. Later additions were made by the Rudolph Steiner School and Alves Village School in Morayshire.

The results were delightful with their humour and originality restoring a faint stir of enthusiasm in Susie for the last stages of the Rainbow Tree project. She began to believe that the vision she had held so long in her heart and mind would indeed become a reality.

Something else happened that summer to re-kindle the excitement of the early years. Vijay, the first of those remarkable Indian children who had given Susie the key to the whole project, came to stay. The fifteen year old had continued to write to her on a regular basis, despite her many changes of address. His cheerful and persistent letters impressed Susie so much that she decided to invite Vijay to come to Scotland for a holiday in the Highland cottage. He accepted with alacrity, persuading his parents to allow him to embark on this adventure and obtaining a visa without difficulty. Susie duly dispatched an air ticket and detailed instructions for the change of terminals at London Airport and the onward flight to Edinburgh. He had the unshakeable confidence of a teenager and arrived in the right place at the right time with a smile of triumph lighting up his face.

The holiday was a huge success. Both the young boy and the older woman became like children, eating ice creams in the rain, making stone gardens on the beach and playing hide and seek in the Ancient Caledonian Wood where some of the oldest trees in Britain still grow. Vijay even volunteered to make an Indian section for the desert patchwork that was later decorated with tartan cacti made by Scottish children.

Susie's search for a property to buy led her and the Indian boy to a small village, situated between the town of Forres and the city of Elgin, in the fertile 'Laich of Moray'. This is a well known agricultural area where there are still a number of family farms working the land, growing barley for the whisky distilleries and rearing cattle and sheep. There are several traditional stone farmhouses, with two or three labourers' cottages opposite them, situated on each side of a narrow lane.

One of these cottages was for sale in the summer of Vijay's holiday. As soon as Susie saw it that she knew that it was what she had been looking for all these years. Memories of childhood holidays at Lossiemouth, in the idyllic days before the second-world war, flooded into her with a sense of welcome. She had come back to her beginning place, or to misquote T.S. Eliot, 'at the end of all her exploring she had come back to the place where she started and was to know it for the first time.'

On October 16, 1998 Susie moved into the farm cottage in Moray. The Cumbrian property had been sold and a small furniture van hired to bring up her belongings. Although smaller in size, her new home seemed to have much more space. There was one large room with high ceilings and an arch in the centre where a wall used to be. Susie had a wood-burning stove installed and spent many hours trying to master the art of keeping it alight all day. Sitting watching the living flames or lying in bed gazing at the glowing embers consumed much of the short days and long nights of the Northern winter.

Having a fire in her bedroom was something she had not had since she was a child. And that was only when she was ill. Susie was not ill, but she was terribly tired and often spent whole days in bed.

There were two proper bedrooms as well as the main room, (where she still chooses to sleep in the cold, dark months of the year), but it was comforting to have the presence of a live fire to keep her company. On sunny days she sometimes sat in the glass box when the afternoon light streamed in to fill the little place with warmth and soothed the aching limbs of her exhausted body. Gradually a healing sense of peace enfolded her as she retreated through time to redeem the innocence of her early life. Perhaps she had come back to discover the light that lived in wee Susie before she lost it when she fell into the dark?

* * *

The woman is not in her box to-day. She is sitting on a rock.

Quite possibly it is the same rock that wee Susie sat upon over sixty years ago, or more likely, scrambled over in a vain attempt to keep up with her brother. He was nine years older than his youngest sister. He could leap from crag to crevice over gushing, sucking gullies of roaring, splashing water without even getting his tennis shoes wet. There was no way that wee Susie could hope to follow him further than the third rock.

This is where the woman sits; on the third rock out to sea.

On this day there are no gushing, sucking, roaring splashes. The stillness of the bright, blue sky has fallen into the sea. Both air and water are transfixed in a breathtaking calm.

Time is suspended in a day that spring forgot to unpack and has dropped into winter.

She cannot move. She too is suspended in time. It is not possible to go on walking.

She has stopped to gaze in bewildered awe across the subdued turquoise expanse stretched out before her. Her eyes are arrested by the border of slate-grey, pink-tinged mountains on the distant north side of the Moray Firth. Her whole being is arrested, compelled to wait upon such transient beauty in silent reverence.

A hush falls upon the entire beach. Dogs hold their bark, walkers whisper to each other and children tiptoe along the sands as if they have wandered into a holy place. But this is no cathedral, no graveyard, no monastery. This is Life in all its majesty and magic.

The only movement is the hypnotic dance of the gentle waves. A deep current, invisible to the eye, pushes up dark, curving slithers of indigo and then, as they curl in upon themselves, the darkness is transformed into light. Creamy, frothy, sparkling bubbles of light run forwards to unfold in lace-edged garlands around the rock, the rock upon which the woman sits with her silent, watching child.

She is beside herself with joy to be back on the beach at Lossiemouth.

* * *

By March 1999 Susie had regained her strength sufficiently to make another trip to Russia. The Millennium was approaching and plans for the final celebrations and the last year of the Rainbow Tree project had to be discussed with her colleagues. She discovered that there was a flight to Moscow from Aberdeen's International Airport, so with the completed sections of the Yellow patchworks in her suitcase and the new Orange designs in her head, Susie set off for her fourth visit to Cheboksary.

As soon as she stepped off the train and onto the familiar station platform she was swept up once again in to the enthusiastic welcome of her Russian friends. It seemed that the whole town had turned out to meet her.

Six schools now participated in the textile project. The work they had produced was superb. A beautiful snow desert scene, painted and embroidered on silk made an impressive contribution to the wilderness triangles and showed that not all deserts were hot. The wild animal piece had a huge moose and fierce black bear that complimented a giant, leaping leopard on one of the Cumbrian sections and a sinister vulture which was of no concern to a jaunty desert fox, in another. Even the border sported a crotchet tortoise, several hand made beaded dragons, a sequin scorpion and may other weird and wonderful beasties. All the schools mounted extensive exhibitions of art, craft and written work related to the themes of wild life and habitats. As always there were wonderful concerts and displays of performing arts that helped to regenerate the creative flow in Susie's energy. She vowed to make a special effort for the final topic of 'Humanity' in the year 2000.

When packing for the journey home, Susie managed to squash both green patchworks as well as the newly assembled yellow ones into her jumbo suitcase. The four pieces were the most cumbersome that had been made and included many three dimensional and stuffed animals as well as a bulbous 'Green Man' complete with a banana moustache and cauliflower ears.

She reckoned it would need four suitcases of similar size to transport the completed series of Rainbow Tree patchworks on the forthcoming Millennium Tour. Although a past master at packing her own 'capsule wardrobes' into a small rucksack, she would certainly need assistance for the final trip next year. At this stage she had no idea how that would come or who would help her but as usual, she assumed God had everything in hand. With this reassuring thought, Susie resolved to commit every resource she had to ensure that the Rainbow Tree project should reach a successful conclusion.

Chapter Eighteen

THE ORANGE SEED

The final stage of the Rainbow Tree was now in sight and Susie's thoughts turned to the launch of the Millennium Exhibition in a year's time. But first she needed to find a way of introducing herself to the community to which she hoped to belong. Sophia, the spinning wheel provided the answer.

On the suggestion of her osteopath, Susie approached the cashmere mill in Elgin with a proposal to demonstrate hand spinning in the newly opened visitor's centre. The proposal was well accepted and an interview with the manager arranged two weeks later. This allowed time to learn the complicated art of spinning cashmere and, wanting to demonstrate her skill as a textile designer as well as craftswoman, Susie made an artistic presentation of yarns and knitted samples. This proved an enjoyable and successful exercise and it was agreed for her to commence regular spinning demonstrations in April 1999.

Susie's new job turned out to be a Godsend. The spinning wheel attracted a great deal of interest from local visitors as well as many tourists from overseas. It was an ideal opportunity to meet people, to make new friends as well as speaking about her work with the Rainbow Tree Project.

A local newspaper article featured a photograph of the former ballet dancer at her spinning wheel and issued an invitation to local schools to join in the making of the Orange patchworks.

Two schools in Alves and Forres responded and Susie started voluntary work in both. A third school in Elgin, with a special interest in growing plants from seed, volunteered to make the missing green border for 'Our Shared Earth'. Appropriately named, 'Greenwards

Primary School' contributed forty-eight individually sewn pieces, delightfully designed by the children themselves to adorn and completed the patchwork.

Susie's next task was to find a venue for the first exhibition of the whole Rainbow Tree series and the final Festival of Friendship in spring 2000. Churches in London and Cumbria had proved ideal places for previous festivals but she wondered if the traditions of the Church of Scotland would allow the same liberties.

St. Giles Church dominated the square in the centre of Elgin. Susie remembered the imposing building from childhood, but had imagined it to be the town hall or some other important secular establishment. The interior, with its circular balcony and high domed ceiling was not dissimilar from St. James Church in Piccadilly that lent itself so well as an exhibition space. Susie decided to attend a Sunday service to investigate the possibility of displaying the Rainbow Tree textile hangings at St. Giles.

The minister was a stirring preacher and his sermon on Psalm Fifteen immediately grabbed her attention. The questions, 'Lord, who may dwell in your sanctuary?' and 'Who may live on your holy hill?' had intrigued her for a long time. The desire to dwell in 'the house of God' had stayed with her since she first heard the idea as a child.

The minister warmed to his theme quoting the psalmist words, 'He whose walk is blameless and does what is righteous, who speaks the truth from his heart and has no slander on his tongue'.

The congregation listened comfortably, seemingly in silent agreement that these qualities were what all good Christians aspired to. It was not until the last verse that an imperceptible rustle of unease swept along the pews.

'He that lends his money without usury will never be shaken.'

The preacher explained that 'in those days' the idea of accruing interest from investments was unheard of and even what we would consider as saving would be thought of as hoarding.

Susie took the text, 'You cannot serve God and money' very seriously and was keen to hear how the apparent difficulty this disparity posed in modern times could be resolved. She was disappointed when the minister sought to reassure the congregation that nowadays things were different and God would not object to the sensible savings and insurance schemes in which most of us invested. We could not be expected to take the Psalmist's words literally.

But Susie had discovered that her 'savings' were a great burden and hindrance when she first lived among the poor in the East End of London. The small legacy she had inherited was not sufficient to live on but was more than the amount of savings allowed if she was to claim State Benefit. She made a vow then always to keep to the limit of three thousand pounds whatever her financial circumstances.

The message from the Psalm seemed clear. She should use the money, set aside to modernise her small, basic kitchen, to finance the Millennium celebrations of the Rainbow Tree.

Immediately a great worry fell from her tense shoulders. Attempts to raise funds to cover the expense of bringing six Russian teachers to Britain for the Festival in 2000 had completely failed. The amount put by for the kitchen was exactly the amount needed for the air fares and Susie felt confident that, if she took responsibility for getting them here, help for accommodation, transport and other aspects of the teacher's visit would be forthcoming.

The next step was to approach the minister at St. Giles. Mr. Rollo listened without comment to Susie's story and her request to hang the exhibition of children's work in the church. He thoughtfully stubbed out his cigarette when she finally stopped speaking.

'How about a Pentecost Festival?' he asked.

This was far more than Susie had hoped for and responding enthusiastically to the suggestion, her imagination began to buzz.

The minister fingered the pictures of the Rainbow Tree patchworks that lay on his desk. 'These look like a creation story to me,' he mused, adding thoughtfully,

'The festival could be spread out over seven days to correspond with the themes of the hangings.'

'Wow!' gasped Susie, 'What a fantastic idea.'

She had certainly found the right place and the right person here.

Mr. Rollo smiled slowly and added casually, 'Actually, my wife is a dance-drama teacher and we often use the Church for performances.'

Susie left his office singing.

Her motivation was now regenerated and enthusiasm for the final pieces of the Rainbow Tree series inspired two complex designs. The 'Tree of Humanity' consisted of eight different branches full of the faces of children. These represented the 'Fruits of Friendship' and took the form of oranges.

'The House of Many Dwellings' was similarly divided, but into a hundred and ninety five six-inch squares rather than a hundred and seventy six circles. Each dwelling was individually made and whether it was a Scottish castle, an igloo, a country cottage, a dacha or a high-rise apartment they were all sewn together into one united house. The entrance was through 'the door of all nations' and the windows were made in Scottish, English, Swedish, Russian and Indian style, by children in all those countries.

Susie worked especially hard in the autumn term of 1999, not only in the local Scottish schools, but also reconnecting with the Cumbria schools and visiting the remaining one on the Isle of Wight. She also sent out detailed instructions, with specially prepared patchwork kits, to the more distant branches. She was determined that their last efforts would be some of the best.

The year 2000 dawned in sparkling sunshine. It was one of those magical winters Susie had dreamed about during her sixteen-year 'exile' in the damp, muggy south. Clear, frosty mornings gave way to the low and brilliant light of short days made all the more beautiful by their poignant brevity. The setting sun painted frozen lochs and bright, white hills with vivid pinks and deep turquoise hues and a whole flock of rare field-fares settled in Susie's garden. It was as if a conference of birds had come from the corners of the earth to help her plan the Festival of Festivals. It may also have had something to do with the heavily laden mountain ash tree that flashed its scarlet bounty in the barren landscape; within a few days the tree was stripped of its berries and the feathered visitors were all gone.

Susie, like the birds, took off to foreign parts. This journey to Russia that March was particularly important and strapping her bulging money belt under the loose travelling sweater, she felt apprehensive. Three thousand crisp, new dollars would not lose touch with Susie's body until she stepped off the train at Cheboksary and could safely hand them over to her Russian friends. The money was their passport to London in five months time. Train tickets for the onward journey to Scotland would be purchased later, by Susie, with the remainder of the 'kitchen money' and posted to Russia prior to the date of departure.

The journey got off to a good start. Aberdeen International Airport was only an hour and a half's drive from Susie's cottage and she relished the relatively tranquil atmosphere of the early morning departure lounge. There was little of the frantic bustle, ceaseless clamour of loud-speaker announcements or nervous restlessness of London Airport. With her precious suitcase safely checked in there was nothing more to worry about until the arrival in Moscow late that afternoon.

Arrive in Moscow she did, but there was no sign of the precious suitcase. The branches of the 'Tree of Humanity' and the 'Dwellings of God's House' were missing. The plane had been delayed at take off and the transferral at Amsterdam Airport was a matter of racing through the vast bewildering building from one gate to another. Susie had imagined her suitcase would have kept up with her rapid change over and was dismayed to discover its absence.

Rita, as always, was there to meet her sister's friend. Yulia was one of the teachers who would come from Cheboksary to Britain in June, so the connection between the two women, now standing together in

Moscow Airport, had deepened considerably. Rita spoke calmly to the official behind the desk. The Russian words exchanged sounded reassuring and the nodding heads and confident smiles directed towards Susie allayed her anxiety. The suitcase would arrive on the early flight to-morrow, the kindly official assured her and he would personally deliver it to the railway station before the train departed for Cheboksary. Her mission of friendship and work with children seemed to have touched the man's heart.

Back at Rita's familiar flat, Susie sank into a soft sea of relief and gratitude. The travel angel was obviously in charge.

Next morning Rita left for work before her guest was awake. There was nothing to do but relax and make the most of this oasis of calm until it was time to go to the station.

Susie was in contemplative mood when sleep receded and the dusty sunlight filtered through her lifting eyelids.

She had been reading T. S. Eliot's 'Four Quartets' on the plane and his words from 'Burnt Norton ' still penetrated her drowsy thoughts.

'To what purpose disturbing the dust on a bowl of rose leaves?' she mused, looking around her. Rita's shabby, old-fashioned apartment had an inexplicable blend of unnoticed chaos and an undisturbed air of tranquillity. Everything was allowed its space and its place was neither dusted nor tidied away. Nothing was arranged in any particular fashion and things just rested peacefully where they had always been.

'To what purpose closing the cupboard door?' Susie asked silently and rhetorically.

What was the point of concealing the comfortable jumble of books, stones, old photographs, a cracked mirror, a timeless clock and a hairbrush? Why bother to disturb the various objects now assuming the permanence of a collection?

Dry leaves, hanging from a seemingly lifeless tree standing in a green plastic bucket, entwined themselves within the majestic antlers of some forgotten moose. Two African masks smiled enigmatically at each other, their noble profiles oblivious of their incongruous environment. A flying turtle defied gravity high on the wall above the hunting trophy, implying a bygone age of activity, while the dust on the faded leaves sprawled silently from the plastic bucket too big to be concealed in a cracked ceramic pot.

Among all this the woman was at peace. The winter sky, devoid of colour, form or movement seemed to shroud the sleeping trees in a maternal embrace. The foolish fantasies, the pointless dusting, the meaningless posturing of mankind were of no concern here. Her extended reverie consumed time and relieved the relentless pace of the journey of her life.

'To what purpose hang the fish upon the line?' she wondered, peering through the grimy window. Her thoughts were, 'they no longer swim and their eyeless sockets are dim,' but the life in which their silver bodies darted and the energy of their aquatic dance was still here. The thread running through all living things was here in the stillness.

The silence pervaded. Containing all sound and yet emitting none, it wrapped its invisible presence around the peeling plaster and endowed the comforting shabbiness with serenity. Accepted and accepting, the unseen guest moved without pressure among the dusty books. No one bothered her, no one bothered about her and she felt completely at home.

Rita's son was somewhere in the flat. Soon he would go to college and Susie would be left alone. Rita said she would come at four o'clock, or later, to make them something to eat. Then they would go to the station and await the errant suitcase.

What might have been and what will be are, at this timeless moment as idle a speculation as 'if suitcases could fly.' Nothing disturbed the traveller sitting on the sagging sofa or the woman working in a city office.

And the narrator in the sunny box knows all will be well.

Chapter Nineteen

THE RED RAY OF HOPE

The narrator had not expected to reach the Red Ray so soon. It was as if the Orange and Red fused together and ran into each other like the flesh of a blood orange.

As Susie said, 'The Red energy of Hope is the hidden force which has motivated us all throughout the entire venture. It will continue to circulate within our lives as long as we believe that we are all part of the world-wide network of creativity that the Rainbow Tree has inspired.'

The eager Russians were ready to go onto the next stage. All six of the schools in Cheboksary, had completed their sections of the Orange patchworks and a workshop had been organised to sew these onto the Scottish pieces Susie had brought with her. The Airport official had not failed her and she had been reunited with the delayed suitcase before the train left Moscow. Once the Russian roof section had been securely attached to the 'House of Many Dwellings' and the top branches of the ' Tree of Humanity' grafted onto the sturdy trunk, it was time to introduce the new design.

The whole exhibition was to be linked by a continuous banner called 'The Red Ray of Hope'. It would not be boxed up into a two-metre square like the twelve other hangings but would consist of innumerable small panels combined to act as a bridge between the old and new millennium. Each one measured rather less than a square metre and consisted of five calico hexagons mounted on a scarlet background.

The ideas for the contents were left entirely up to the great diversity of adults and children who made more than fifty panels for the Red Ray during the coming year.

The first ones were started during Susie's visit to Cheboksary and served to keep up the momentum until the Summer Festival in Britain.

The excitement was intense. Only one of the six teachers (apart from Yelena) had ever been outside Russia. The forthcoming trip was a chance of a lifetime. All the preparatory work was in place. The three thousand dollars were safely deposited in the bank until they were needed to purchase airfares, visas and train tickets to Moscow. Rehearsals for the dance drama had been held and arrangements for the Festival programme finalised during the last few days of Susie's visit.

A mood of celebration permeated the farewell party that was a traditional part of all her visits. It was as usual, hosted by the owner of the best restaurant in town. Music and dancing and innumerable toasts were essential ingredients of all Russian parties, whether the venue was a fishing lodge beside the river Volga, a fourth floor apartment in a concrete block, an artist's studio (provided by the State) or a banqueting hall of faded grandeur. It was impossible not to be swept up in the spirit of generosity and energetic enjoyment that kept everyone eating, drinking, singing and dancing long into the night. Susie's one toast, 'Lubov & Druzbha' (Love and Friendship), always delighted these exuberant people who had taken her so warmly into their hearts. Her Russian was still limited to a few words and phrases but she did her best to deliver them with the stylish panache of her friends.

The real work began as soon as Susie returned home. Her small cottage was overwhelmed with the remaining 'branches' and 'dwellings' that came in by post from Sweden, Cumbria and the Isle of Wight. Numerous 'Red Ray' kits were waiting to be cut out and distributed to the many people who were keen to join the last stage of a the textile project. The simple theme of 'Hope' captured the imagination of the tourists and holidaymakers who heard about the Rainbow Tree Festival from Susie while she was spinning at the cashmere mill. The small panels were easily portable and many found their way to distant countries like South Africa, New Zealand and America.

There were now just three weeks left before the opening exhibition of the Rainbow Tree's Millennium Tour on April 22 at Elgin Library. Susie was reminded of the total dedication required when she had to complete her Exhibition of Visionary Altar Hangings for St. James' Piccadilly for the opening presentation on August 6, 1991. This final task had to take priority over everything else, including her living space.

She cleared as much furniture from the cottage's main room as possible and brought the large art table in from the sunny box.

Although the traveller had found her home, she retained a flexible and simple style of living and the rooms were required to adapt to whatever was needed at the time. Sophia, the spinning wheel had to work overtime; three days a week demonstrating fine spinning of exotic fibres, such as cashmere, camel, guanaco, alpaca, mohair and silk, and in the evenings blending hand spun rough, thickly textured yarns into twigs and branches for the 'Tree of Humanity'. There were also yards and yards of hand- made orange braid to be twisted and turned and created into borders for the ' bricks and mortar' that held all the dwellings in the 'House' together.

The Orange patchworks were cumbersome and unwieldy to work with and taxed her strength to the limit but the enchanting efforts of all the children touched Susie deeply. The sea of faces seemed to epitomise our crowded world and yet there was still room for everyone to share the common source of hope growing up from the trunk of the new tree. Every tiny image of a human home seemed to have had a place prepared for it in God's House and wee Susie seemed to look over her shoulder, exclaiming she could see little lights shining out of all the windows.

By the end of three punishing weeks, all twelve patchworks were ready to be hung. Many of them had required some restoration but all had survived their extensive journeying remarkably well. The completed Rainbow Tree Exhibition filled the entire wall space of the art gallery in Elgin Library. The new building was situated in the middle of the city's fine park and was a popular venue for exhibitions and a wide variety of events. As a tribute to Susie's educational artwork with children, the council made the generous gesture of allowing the Rainbow Tree to be displayed free of charge. Members of the staff were immensely encouraging and the caretaker, who helped Susie to hang the exhibition, even managed to attach the original sixteen by fourteen feet collage from the ceiling in some ingenious way. Its worn and travel-stained presence still told a visual story of how the whole seven-year venture had begun.

The overall effect was stunning. The colours of the rainbow took on new depths as they radiated around the gallery and the individual pieces blended into a cohesive whole. Here indeed was a contemporary creation myth which demonstrated the spirit of human creativity in a truly vibrant and innovative way.

Susie's big brother was the first of her family to see the Exhibition. It helped to explain and put in context what she had been doing over the past years of frantic travelling and many house moves. As well as being suitably and genuinely impressed, the retired general was surprised to notice how the boating pond, beside the library, had shrunk since youthful holidays. He remembered a vast and treacherous lake of unfathomable depths where he had heroically rowed his younger sister to safety through storms, monsters and gales.

Susie's eldest sister also made the effort to come up to see the opening presentation at St. Giles Church a few weeks later. She and her husband sat beaming, in the front row, watching her dance just as they had done over forty years ago when she gave a charity performance in Inverness. It didn't matter that there were very few others in the rows behind, the display of loyalty and support from her siblings meant more to Susie than a packed house.

There were three other 'trailer exhibitions' in the smaller towns of

Keith, Buckie and Forres, following the highly successful opening month in Elgin. These helped to generate interest and herald the main Festival in June. All the arrangements for the four-week programme in Scotland and the Lake District depended solely on Susie. She was still a one-woman band and did everything from booking train seats, driving the mini-bus, organising public presentations and school visits to choreographing a dance-drama and writing the script for the final event at Cartmel Priory in Cumbria.

Although she had attended St. Giles church regularly since the end of 1998, Susie had failed to entice much support for the Rainbow Tree Festival. She was a newcomer to these parts and the unusual nature of her work must have been difficult for many people to relate to. Something more relevant to the traditions of the church was needed to engage the interest and involvement of the congregation.

An idea came to Susie. She asked the minister's permission to design a special banner for St. Giles to mark Pentecost and to invite the ladies of the Church Guild to help her make it.

Once again his reply was surprising. 'We could do with a new cloth for the communion table.'

Susie had not expected to be entrusted with something so sacred and felt honoured by the minister's faith in her ability. The ladies responded enthusiastically to the project and a sewing group was immediately arranged. Interest in the children's patchworks and a sense of communal involvement generated encouragingly during the weekly sessions and Susie felt welcomed into the bosom of the Kirk.

The Pentecost Rainbow Tree Festival opened on Sunday, June 4, 2000. The whole exhibition hung from the gallery all around the church. The central focus was the silk cloth on the communion table, radiantly embroidered with a huge golden goblet overflowing with tongues of fire made in the shape of teardrops. The hanging, which had heralded the Rainbow Tree vision in 1992, called the 'Eternal Seed', was draped from the pulpit above. It showed a broken heart-shaped seed burning like a ball of flames transforming pain into life-giving love and new growth. There was a special service to dedicate all the work to the glory of God and to pray for His blessings during the following week.

Then the Russians arrived. Pritiben, the Indian co-ordinator had also made the effort to come to Scotland for the final celebrations of the project to which she had contributed so much. Susie's cottage expanded to accommodate the seven guests, six of whom would stay until the beginning of July. Out came the flexible floor cushions to serve as seating and bedding as on previous Festivals of Friendship. The 'girls' had no problem in settling in immediately and were far too excited by their first glimpses of Britain to feel any ill effects from the three-day journey. This included a day's sightseeing in London and an overnight stay in the Y.W.C.A. hostel before the eight-hour train journey to Inverness. . There was much 'talking in the dorm' long after Susie had put her light out and fallen fast asleep.

Next morning, the group set off for Elgin to see the end result of the work of which they were all a part and to celebrate whole Rainbow Tree Exhibition for the first time.

All around the church hung the Rainbow Tree patchworks filling the entire space. Each day of the following week children rushed into the austere building with unbridled excitement to celebrate their own and each other's work.

* * *

A WHOLE NEW STORY OF CREATION WAS ABOUT TO BEGIN

ON MONDAY, 'THE PLANETS' WERE CREATED OUT OF PURPLE SPACE.

On that day, the tiny pre-primary children from Rose Brae School came to open proceedings with a magical star dance and to see the Red Ray of Hope they had filled with brilliant, beaded hearts. They marked the beginning and the end of the project.

ON TUESDAY, 'AQUATIC LIFE' WAS CREATED OUT OF INDIGO WATER.

On that day, pupils from Alves primary School brought Mums and Dads and Aunties and Grannies to exclaim at the extent and skill of the many pieces made by their talented offspring and to join in singing 'It's Time for Us All to Sing One Song'.

ON WEDNESDAY, 'BIRDS of TRAVEL' WERE CREATED OUT OF BLUE AIR.

On that day, a crowd of rather bewildered children from Seafield School was brought into the church by the St. Giles' youth-worker. They had not taken part in the textile project and did not seem to understand why they were here, but as soon as they saw the dazzling display they joined into the spirit of celebration.

ON THURSDAY, 'THE PLANTS' WERE CREATED OUT OF GREEN EARTH.

On that day, nearly fifty children from Greenwards School proudly displayed their designs for the border of the Russian patchwork and recited poems about vegetables and flowers. Posies from the school garden enhanced the lunch-time service with a special grace.

ON FRIDAY, 'THE ANIMALS' WERE CREATED OUT OF YELLOW DESERTS.

On that day children from the Moray Stiener school arrived from Forres, dressed all in white. They gave a moving performance of how, in their imagination, the earth and all living creatures came into being. They concluded the celebration by passing a lighted candle from child to child, adult to adult, all around the church. As each handed the living flame on, everyone said the name of the next recipient in unison. This ritual was something the children often practised in their school but was a completely new experience for most of the congregation. The church was learning from the little children how to become as young at heart and simple in spirit as it was in the beginning.

ON SATURDAY, 'HUMANITY' WAS CREATED OUT OF ORANGE FLESH.

On that day, the Russian teachers gave a presentation of national dances, songs and poetry from their native Chuvashia in gorgeous red and white costumes and elaborately embellished head-dresses. The second part of the programme was a performance of the 'Original Seed' dance-drama led by Susie. She had made brand new robes for the four 'Elements' and 'Humanity', portrayed by her brave colleagues. Yelena narrated the script with customary verve and style and was resplendent in a shimmering red sheath.

Pritiben welcomed members of the audience in a fabulous silk sari and traditional Indian courtesy. She opened the event, as she had done six years ago in St. James' Church, London, with a Hindu chant. Its ancient and holy sound transcended all religious differences into one eternal voice.

ON SUNDAY, 'THE SPIRIT of HOPE' WAS CREATED OUT OF RED ENERGY.

On this day, the Festival of Pentecost was celebrated by the whole congregation.

The minister's sermon was inspired, the choir sang lustily, the overseas' visitors were introduced, the children of the Sunday School decked the pulpit in red, yellow and orange paper flames suspended precariously from bendy curtain rails, the people joined in the spirit of celebration and above the whole assembly hung the Rainbow Tree Exhibition in all its glory. It was glorious, indeed, to have brought into being the vision that Susie had held for so long and the children had made real. This was the real spirit of Pentecost, a living witness for all to see and believe in.

* * *

The following three days after the opening festival allowed a little respite before the next presentation of the exhibition in the visitors' centre at the cashmere mill. Susie was gaining confidence as a bus driver and took delight in showing her guests the beautiful countryside of the Highlands of Scotland as well as transporting them on visits to local schools. Everyone was charmed by the Indian and Russian teachers and impressed by their grasp of the English language and knowledge of contemporary history and customs. Exchange of national dances, poetry and songs were enthusiastically received and given from both sides.

A presentation at Johnston's Mill was also a great success and several invitations were issued to the group as a result; including a haggis supper, morning coffee and afternoon tea. The social programme was filling all the gaps in between a workshop at Aberlour preparatory school, assembly at Gordonstoun School, an inter-faith service in the ruins of Elgin Cathedral, a presentation at the Universal hall at the Findhorn Foundation and a display at the Moray Steiner School. The highlight of the visit to Scotland was a wonderful concert of the complete Chopin Nocturnes given by Benjamin Frith in a country house hotel in the ancient town of Nairn.

The farewell party in Susie's modest cottage lacked the space and grandeur of the Russian restaurant, but the singing, dancing and feasting were no less exuberant. Friends packed the living room, the kitchen and the adjoining sunny box (as the Russians had christened the square, glass porch). Everyone was everyone's best friend and there was no barrier of class, culture, language or creed to hinder the high spirits, laughter and joy. This was one of those times when human beings realised that the command to 'love one another' is not impossible and that the only 'enemy,' preventing us from doing so, is imprisoned within ourselves.

Next morning, Saturday July the first, the Rainbow Tree group headed south. They were on the way to Bankfoot, near Perth, for the next Festival. The mini bus had now been returned to the hire firm but the generosity of Mr Arnold Clark, who had lent it to the group free of charge, was still greatly appreciated by all concerned. He even turned a blind eye to the very small scratch the driver had incurred trying to manoeuvre around the corner of the narrow lane behind her cottage. Now it was the job of Hector, (Susie's small car), to transport the hangings on the next stage of the Millennium tour. As there was room for only the driver and two passengers the rest of the party had to travel by bus to Perth. There Susie's sister and brother-in-law met them and the whole party was reunited in a roadside restaurant at a sumptuous lunch hosted by this generous couple.

The Rainbow Tree group proceeded to the little stone church in the village of Bankfoot to prepare for the festival. The congregation were hosting a visit from a number of children from Chernobyl and the idea was to link the two Russian groups together with Red Rays of Hope. Each had made panels to add to the growing banner and this would be the main theme for a celebration service next day.

Soon the church was decked with colour and the hangings emerged as vibrant as ever from the boot of the small car. The Red Rays hung above the communion table and made a striking centrepiece. The minister and his wife, and indeed the whole community welcomed Susie's group with exceptional warmth. A marquee had been erected in the manse gardens, a large buffet provided and guest bedrooms made ready for the night. Singing and dancing in both Scottish and Russian style created an atmosphere that made everyone feel at home.

When the time came for the Rainbow Tree group to depart after the extraordinary Sunday Festival there were tearful farewells among the warm hugs and promises to keep in touch.

The next port of call was Cartmel, in the Lake District. Vijay had just arrived at Manchester Airport from India, having been delayed twice due to problems in acquiring a visa. This meant his original plan to travel up to Moray for the Elgin festival had had to be cancelled and last minute alternative arrangements had to be made. The headmistress of Beetham primary school kindly agreed to meet and take care of him until Susie and the other visitors arrived from Scotland and elsewhere.

A large Swedish group, who had participated in the last three years of the Rainbow Tree project, had also come to the Millennium celebrations to meet their Cumbrian pen friends. Accommodation was scarce and with such a large influx descending on the pupils and staff of the tiny village school help was needed.

The new Dean of Cartmel Priory and his wife came to her rescue. They not only received guests into their own home but also persuaded their parishioners to do the same. The vicar even arranged for a jolly couple to drive up to Perthshire to collect Susie and the Russians and once again strangers became friends overnight.

The five days spent in the picturesque village of Cartmel was one of the highlights of the month and made a fitting finale to the whole trip. The ancient Priory Church was an impressive venue for the exhibition of children's work. Fortunately, one of the wardens was a civil engineer and had asked for the measurements to be sent to him in advance in order to make preparations to hang the patchworks. He had constructed a series of wooden batons to fit snugly between the high stone pillars holding up the huge building and two props with which to hoist the twelve heavy hangings up to their lofty position.

The Rainbow Tree itself was slung above the elaborately carved altar screen, by an ingenious system of ropes and pulleys, directly in front of a magnificent stained glass window. The light shone through the threadbare fabric, endowing it with an ethereal beauty and transformed its battered appearance into one of tender grace.

Susie was greatly moved by the special efforts made to display the exhibition, particularly by someone who had no personal connection with the project. It seemed that those who had 'eyes to see' and understood the vision of the Rainbow Tree instantly became, or perhaps already were, a part of it. The lonely burden of carrying the project was swept away in the warmth of its conclusion.

Susie's joy was complete when her middle sister, who had watched and supported her through her early performing career, came up from Cheshire to see the exhibition and the final presentation of the 'Original Seed' dance-drama.

This had grown from a one women act to a huge event with 'a cast of thousands'. The lone figure, poised in the Void of the Beginning was gradually joined by more and more characters until it seemed the whole of creation filled the aisles with sound and movement.

The Cumbrian Schools contributed their own interpretations of Water, Air and Earth, with pupils dressed in specially designed costumes including a giant model of the 'Green Man'. The Swedes wore fantastic masks of Wild Animals and the Russians' red and white national dresses made a splendid splash for Humanity.

Then came the Red Ray of Hope. The grand finale was led by Vijay, dressed in simple white cotton, hand woven in his native village. The boy stood alone in front of the high altar. Holding the roll of red cloth in his slender, dark hands, he began to walk slowly forwards, gradually gathering all the other young people behind him. The long banner unwound from the leader's hands until the whole procession carried it aloft like a blazing, scarlet path weaving its way through the middle of the church.

Susie's voice rang out with the words,

'Even now, all over the world, flames are flickering,
Leaping from heart to heart with the light of Hope.
Whoever you are, wherever you live,
Whatever you do, however you pray,
There is Hope in each one of us.
There is hope in this one language which we all understand,
This language without words which unites us through sorrow and joy,
Beyond distance and space,
Before life and after death.'

Then, in a moment of silence, the young carriers of the Red Ray of Hope turned to face the assembled company.

With one voice, echoing around the huge building, they all cried in unison:

'ITS NAME IS LOVE.'

Chapter Twenty

THE FRUITS OF THE RAINBOW TREE

The Pentecost Tree is Christ's answer to The Suffering Tree, wrote Susie to the director of St. Mungo Museum of Religious Art and Life. She proposed to base her design for a Christian banner for the millennium on a format used to powerful effect in a work made for a vigil for the homeless at Westminster Abbey in 1992. The theme, then, had been the dispossessed all over the world; the ethnically cleansed in Bosnia, the Kurdish refugees, the flood victims of Bangladesh, the cardboard box community living under the arches of Waterloo Station.

Photographs of faces filled the branches of the 'Suffering Tree'. Each was tenderly enfolded in a hand-spun 'twig' that grew from the compassionate sap giving life and healing to the brokenness of humanity. Making the banner was an act of creative meditation requiring no words to reach deeply into the hearts of all those who cut out and brought newspaper photographs for the spinner to weave into the tree.

When Susie was commissioned to make the Millennium banner for the Glasgow Museum, she had no hesitation in deciding the new theme.

She had already researched the Pentecost phenomenon thoroughly in order to extract from her thoughts, the design for the St. Giles' communion tablecloth. The opportunity to develop this into a larger and more substantial work came as a welcome surprise. It was exciting enough when the director of the prestigious Museum had responded so enthusiastically when Susie first approached him about the Rainbow Tree project. His recommendation to Glasgow Council that

173

they should fund an exhibition of the hangings was readily accepted and arrangements made for it to occupy the gallery space for three months directly after the Festival in Cartmel Priory.

This had come as a great boost to the exhausted co-ordinator. Susie could now hand over all the responsibility for all the practical organisation to the professional staff of St. Mungo's and become an artist again. She was certainly treated like one. On several visits to the Museum Gallery, to open the exhibition with dance and story telling and for a reception with local dignitaries, then later, to give a press conference and an introductory talk about the new commission, Susie Rose, (as the artist was addressed), revelled in the luxury of staying in a hotel and having all her expenses paid by someone else. The public recognition of her work as a textile artist gave Susie the incentive to look to the future with new hope.

It might have been a terrible anti-climax when the Russians suddenly departed at the end of the celebrations but, as Vijay's visa was extended for a month's holiday he provided company as well as help in dismantling the exhibition before taking it to Glasgow.

On returning home there was no time to waste before starting on the Pentecost Tree.

It was an ambitious and elaborate work. A painted silk background, measuring two square metres, presented a vivid image of ocean shapes in blues, purples and greens. Attached to this was a traced map of the world without boundaries made from pale apple green gauze. Thrusting up from the depths of the sea, with its roots reaching to the far corners and spilling over the edge of the cloth, was the Pentecost Tree. It flung out its branches, like the arms of the cross, over the whole Earth.

Bursting through the top was the Risen Life of Christ, symbolised by a fiery ball of flames. Even the dead tree, bearing the body of the crucified Son of Man, had been revived by the power of the Holy Spirit.

Part of the terms of the commission stated that members of

Glasgow's local community should be involved in creating the Millennium banner. To meet this criteria, Susie made sixty two 'leaf' kits, including hand dyed and spun silk embroidery threads, which were eagerly taken up by volunteers. When the whole piece was completed, the act of sewing the leaves onto the 'Pentecost Tree' inspired the same sense of unity which had empowered the 'Suffering Tree'.

Now the fruits of shared sorrow and pain had become the flame-like leaves which were for 'the healing of the nations'.

One tree seemed to grow out of another. The progression was continuous from the 'Tree of Knowledge' to the 'Tree of Life', both central to the myths of many religious and sacred traditions. In between these two archetypal giants was a whole host of themes encompassing and inspiring parables, stories, dramas and images related to trees. The Rainbow Tree was like a contemporary myth and, like the Tree of Life, was bearing fruit of many kinds.

Already it was September. Preparations for the Easter Festival at the completion of the Exhibition's Millennium tour had begun in Cheboksary and Susie was asked to send details for a final design to mark the special occasion.

The description of the Tree of Life in the last book of the Bible, with twelve different kinds of fruit and leaves, for the 'healing of the nations' seemed ideal. The Russians teachers had each been given, by the minister of Bankfoot Church, illustrated children's Bibles in their own language. The text could be the inspiration for each group to interpret in their own way.

Susie invited local schools to take part in making a Scottish Tree of Life and other banners for the Easter festival in 2001. She hoped the involvement of children might help her to find at least three adults to assist in transporting the textile exhibition to Russia.

It worked!

Two Sunday school teachers from St. Giles and another from a new Community Church in Elgin volunteered to accompany her on the epic journey. The Primary Schools volunteered to make the 'New Tree of Life', and several other Sunday Schools agreed to make more panels for the 'Everlasting Red Ray of Hope'. Wherever the Rainbow Tree went it inspired the creative instincts in those who saw what little children could do and the bridging banner continued to expand.

The Easter Festival in Russia seemed a true symbol of unity. Unlike most years, the highlight of the Christian Calendar fell on the same date in 2001. The Eastern Orthodox and the Western branches of the Church were not, as usual, separated by a week's distance but would celebrate Easter together on April 15. What had been rent apart by disagreeing priests in the schism of the eleventh century would be united 2000 years after the original event.

If this was not a sign from God, it was certainly an extremely auspicious day upon which to celebrate the Rainbow Tree and its fruits made by children in both East and West.

Meanwhile the exhibition was on its travels again.

Edinburgh was its next destination. It was with a sense of anticipation that Susie approached her old school, St. George's. She had left, at the age of thirteen, under the cloud of the then headmistress's disapproval. To give up the superior educational opportunities of one of the best schools in Scotland for the doubtful pursuit of ballet dancing was not something the scholarly woman could endorse. She considered this passion of Susie's 'a temporary phase', which in her judgement was unwise to encourage.

Now the former pupil had returned. Not only with a successful ballet career to her credit, but also with an international textile exhibition recently shown and widely acclaimed in Glasgow. Old rivalries between the two great cities still lurked beneath the veneer of polite facades but there was a mutual respect for the arts in both. The dancer-artist was determined to find venues in her hometown to provide comparable time and space to display her work.

A joint exhibition was arranged in collaboration with the school's impressive art department to exhibit the St. George's Millennium banner and the Rainbow hangings in the assembly hall. The vast wood panelled room had not changed since wee Susie used to sit cross-legged on the floor at the front with the insignificant juniors at weekly gatherings. Never in her wildest dreams did she ever have the audacity to imagine that one day she would sit on the stage next to the head as an honoured guest. She had been taken completely by surprise, when, having waited a week to meet the revered and stately Dr. McClure, the art mistress grabbed her minutes before the Friday Assembly.

'Now is your chance', the teacher whispered, pushing Susie forward as the head made her way towards the hall door.

Introduced as the designer of the visiting exhibition, the former pupil found herself looking up to the beaming face of a gowned figure towering above her.

'Marvellous, marvellous,' boomed the welcoming voice, glancing around the hangings in the hall.

'Would you like to speak to the school now, instead of my usual address?' Dr. McClure asked.

'Of course,' gulped Susie, as she followed the entourage striding through rows of waiting girls.

With no time to think, she rose to the occasion feeling a wave of excitement fill her being. The child danced inside her grown-up self. 'Wee Susie' had become 'Susie Rose'. Her voice rang out with undisguised exuberance as she described, in the allotted five minutes, the intense joy of being here at this moment.

The Rainbow Tree patchworks filled the old hall with the colours of Life and demonstrated what can be achieved without the aid of a maths 'O' level, a university degree, a lottery grant or even a formal art training.

The small sixty-something, former ballet dancer told her young audience, 'Everything you need for life is within each one of you, just waiting be unlocked, like treasure in a box.'

The head mistress looked at her guest in a moment of recognition and on the spur of the moment invited the guest to 'come to lunch'.

Over the elegant meal, attended by members of the art staff and the rather bewildered rector of one of Glasgow's top Academies, (who had come expecting to discuss educational reform), the conversation revolved around the Rainbow Tree.

Realising that Susie had run the project on faith alone and had always responded to a challenge, Dr. McClure suddenly asked, 'Will you go to Pushkin?'

'Of course', laughed Susie, 'I'd go to the moon if I was asked.'

She had no idea where Pushkin was but it sounded promising and she always leapt at any opportunity to further her work and make new contacts.

It turned out there was a church and Sunday school in this famous suburb of St. Petersburg which had a special significance for St. George's through links formed by a Russian pupil and her parents. Dr. McClure had a personal love of the Orthodox liturgy and had visited Pushkin herself. She was keen to develop the relationship with the Russian priests who ran the church school and wondered if the Rainbow Tree project might act as an intermediary. It seemed an exciting prospect.

Leaving her old school with promises to keep in touch and with a letter already dispatched to Pushkin, Susie did not have far to go for the next stage of the Millennium Tour. St. Mary's Episcopal Cathedral was situated in the West End of Edinburgh and had already staged an exhibition of her 'Visionary Altar Hangings' during the summer of 1992. The Provost extended the same warmth and trust to the Rainbow Tree as he had shown during her first visit when he had offered the space of the Resurrection Chapel.

The Rainbow Tree had grown far beyond the capacity of the side chapel and spilled out along the entire length of the North wall, but although this caused some surprise, the Cathedral community generously received the children's work into their midst. It brought unexpected colour and light to the grey month of November and the renowned music and singing of St. Mary's Cathedral seemed to bestow a new blessing upon the patchworks.

In the month of her sixty-fifth birthday Susie felt she had come back to the place of her birth to be received as the whole woman she was becoming. The journey of her transformation was nearly completed.

Chapter Twenty One

EASTER IN RUSSIA

The Rainbow Tree Exhibition was ahead of the four women who were busily preparing to take it to Russia. It had travelled without Susie's aid to the Lake District since leaving Edinburgh at the beginning of December 2000. An Exhibition had been organised by the art teacher of John Ruskin School many of whose pupils had made important contributions to the textiles. Surely the great nineteenth century artist and educational philosopher, from whom the school took its name, would have approved of such an innovative demonstration of some of his beliefs.

It was now the first month of the first year of the third Millennium and the Rainbow Tree had reached London. Susie had travelled down by train to catch up with the exhibition. Four large laundry bags, deposited at St. James' Church by a courier firm, were waiting to be unpacked. The familiar task of hanging large pieces of heavily decorated pieces of cloth from the balconies presented no problems. Ten years after her first exhibition in the famous Christopher Wren building, the 'artist for God' felt immensely privileged to have the fruits of her labours so prominently displayed once again.

The month in central London offered the opportunity for many old friends and colleagues to re-connect with the spinner-dancer-artist who they remembered as a vivid part of the diverse community of the unusual church. She stayed 'in residence' until the beginning of February when the Rainbow Tree exhibition was transferred to All Saints Church in Battersea.

This small, modern church had a strong connection with India and the style of worship included many Eastern customs. Children played an important role, reading the lessons in loud, clear voices and participating in processions, prayers and rituals throughout every service. Contemporary and traditional art was also encouraged as valid examples of visual prayer and some of the early Rainbow Tree hangings had already been displayed on previous occasions. Everyone was eager to see the latest works, 'The House of Many Dwellings', 'The Tree of Humanity' and the 'Red Rays of Hope'. The latter was of special interest as it included a new panel made by Ella, a staunch member of All Saints Church. Leaving the exhibition in the trusty hands of the two priests in charge, Susie returned home to Scotland to prepare for the final trip to Russia.

The Rainbow Tree would make two more showings, on the Isle of Wight at the Quay Arts Centre and in a gallery in Cornwall, before she would see it again. Complex arrangements had been made by friends, fans and colleagues to collect, transport, transfer and deliver the textiles from place to place. Everything was done on trust. There were no insurance policies, no guarantees (written or otherwise), no money exchanged, just a mutual faith in the vision of the project and implicit trust in each other.

The plan was that at the end of its tour of the South, the Exhibition would be deposited at the flat of someone's brother in Chiswick. The fact that none of the three people involved knew each other and two had no previous links with the project did not cause any of them to hesitate in committing themselves and their resources to this unusual and demanding venture. A series of small miracles accompanied the Rainbow Tree wherever it went. Across the wintry sea, in a dreary motorway café and through areas stricken with 'foot and mouth' disease, it opened up paths of hope in the bleak early months of 2001.

The 'someone', who had a brother in Chiswick, was Jo, one of the three women who was preparing to come to Russia. Brother Bill was quite simply an angel. Not only did he put his luxurious, riverside flat at the disposal of his sister's friend's friends, but also acted as custodian for the vast exhibition and as chauffeur for all the visits to and from airports. With help like this it was much easier to organise the end of the Millennium tour than it had been at the beginning.

Susie persuaded Jo, June and Jane to pack 'capsule wardrobes' in overnight cases and keep the large suitcases, each of them would take, empty until they reached London. They practised by squeezing three double duvets and two small quilts into the four cases reckoning that these were equivalent to the dimensions of the series of textiles they had to haul across Russia. Personal belongings had to be kept to the minimum and everyone prayed for the thaw to come early that year. There was no room for fur coats although June insisted in carrying one over her arm. 'To give to a needy person,' she said. A few weeks later, in the sweating metropolis of Moscow, this extra burden would be the cause of both regret and mirth.

Jane's idea was Scottish country dancing. 'We should demonstrate something from our culture,' she said. As none of them felt up to reciting Burns, about whose poetry the Russians were far more knowledgeable than many Scots, and bagpipes were out of the question, it was agreed to dance a Foursome Reel.

Memories of Saturday night dances in the Marine Hotel, Lossiemouth came to Susie as soon as the Strathspey music began. She had been too young, at the time, to be allowed to join in but a vision of her eldest sister dancing to the elegant reel floated into her mind. She tried to hold her imaginary skirt with the same grace as her teenage sibling.

They would have to have skirts, said June. 'And sashes', added Jane. She often attended Scottish Dance Seminars and liked to have things done properly. Jo was a new comer to the reels, which were a familiar part of the other three's childhoods, but smiled winningly to disguise an occasional slight shuffling of the feet. The rehearsals were an important part of the group 'bonding' before they embarked on their epic journey. There were four overnight train journeys ahead during which the women would have to share a sleeping berth, and it was advisable to get to know each other as well as possible in advance.

On Thursday, March 29, sixty people crammed into Birnie village hall to bid the four travellers a hearty farewell. Mission F.I.S.H (Friends In Spirit and Hope), as the venture was named, had attracted a great deal of support from the local community. Susie's companions were all well-known and popular figures in and around Elgin and had many well-wishers to send them on their way. There was an impressive display of small banners and needlework specially made as gifts to take to Russia. A new logo, designed to mark the unique meeting of East and West at Easter, had two symbolic fish facing each other with overlapping heads. The one visible eye showed, Susie explained, that we were all one in the eye of God.

Next day she travelled alone to London. The others would join her on April 5, on the evening before the flight to Moscow. She took with her the 'New Tree of Life', jointly made by three groups of Scottish children in Moray and Edinburgh, to be displayed at an International Service of Unity at All Saint's church, Battersea. It had been planned, during Susie's February visit, to dedicate the new work and to give her a blessing for the Russian trip. The moving ceremony strengthened her spirit and gave her moral support for the final stage of the Rainbow Tree.

Arriving at Brother Bill's flat on the morning before 'take off', she was relieved to see the familiar bags waiting in the entrance hall. They had been delivered, according to plan, from Cornwall via the Isle of Wight. Bill showed his sister's friend into his spacious drawing room with French windows opening out into an elegant riverside garden. It was on the opposite bank from the company house to which the director had taken his ballerina bride to nearly forty -two years ago. The young wife had often pushed her babies along the towpath and sat on the seat facing the gracious old house now receiving the mature woman.

* * *

All her life is gathering within her. Nothing has been lost. No part of it has totally died. Each stage has given something living in her at this moment. The past is growing like a healthy tree, budding from the scars of pruning. The Rainbow Tree has served as a vehicle for the journey which has brought together all the separate fragments now making up the whole woman. She feels gratitude for the benefits of her married life and the babies who have grown up to develop talents from both their parents. Daughter and son have successfully blended the qualities of father and mother, combining art and design with a flair for business and music with teaching skills and a love of sailing. As the woman in the drawing room looks across the river at the reflection of her early self, she pauses and gives thanks for everything life has bestowed upon her.

* * *

But this was not the time for contemplation.

'Make yourself at home,' Bill's voice brought the dreamer back to the particular point of time in which she stood.

'Feel free,' he went on, 'to use this room as your own.'

The generous man indicated two jumbo sofas that would act as beds for the 'girls' when they arrived from Inverness that evening. Susie welcomed his permission to unpack the contents of the waiting bags and spread them out all over the deep pile carpet. The hangings seemed to have grown. They looked far bigger than the representative duvets and quilts and she wondered how on earth they would fit into the four allotted suitcases. The trick was to fold them like those sleeping bags which disappear into impossibly small nylon bags, or rain coats supposed to fit into their own pockets. She had not yet mastered the skills her son performed with enviable ease, but now was the time to try.

One by one, she laid the patchworks flat on the floor. Carefully smoothing each crease out, patting every bulge down and stretching all the edges taught, she folded them like the linen sheets which used to fill her mother's airing cupboard. Then, removing her shoes, Susie trod out the last remaining air pockets with strong practised feet. It became a little dance.

'Eight steps to the right, eight steps to the left, turn to face the window and repeat in the other direction.'

She hummed a distant tune from Brahms, used for the Grade Four ballet exam, then changed it to something more lively.

'Jump, two, three, four and step hop, seven eight, to the left, two three four and finish feet together', she chanted, not quite under her breath, because Bill came in to see if she was all right.

By lunchtime, three immaculately folded bundles stood neatly on the drawing room carpet. The fourth and biggest bundle was already securely packed into Susie's suitcase. This encouraging omen would, she hoped, help to convince her companions that they could accommodate the others in their luggage.

A less encouraging omen was the flight from Inverness being delayed three times. It was after eight when the three 'Jays' arrived at Luton airport. Bill and his first guest met the weary travellers in his elevated 'people-carrier' and with characteristic and decisive generosity, Jo's brother whisked them all off to his favourite Indian restaurant for a meal. By the time they finally reached the Chiswick flat, a mood of relaxed excitement oiled the re-arranging of luggage and four tightly zipped suitcases stood like stuffed hippopotami by the front door before their packers fell into an instant sleep upon the sumptuous sofas.

The early morning flight to Moscow proceeded according to plan and it was not until the Rainbow Tree group emerged from the dingy customs and immigration hall that the first problem arose. There was no sign of Rita, or her husband or any one else Susie could recognise. The foreigners stood in a helpless huddle and wished they had studied their Russian phrase books more closely. Their attempts to explain their predicament to the solemn faced airport official were greeted with a stream of incomprehensible words and gestures. There was nothing to do but to sit and wait and hope someone would eventually come to meet them.

Now two hours later, the four foreign women (it was always a humbling experience to feel like an alien so soon after leaving home) sat upon a different bench in another vast, echoing area full of hurrying people who knew exactly where they were going. This was one of Moscow's several railway stations and they were waiting hopefully to board a night train to St. Petersburg. These were many and frequent but as it was the start of the Easter holidays, large Russian families crowded onto the platforms and swarmed onto every train as soon as it had disgorged the incoming passengers.

Someone did indeed come to meet them. Rita's husband had been taken ill and the mother of the friend of someone's daughter had nobly taken his place at the last minute. Svetlana had escorted the cumbersome group from one side of the traffic-riddled city to the other and when the huge suitcases challenged the disgruntled bus driver, she engaged in a heated argument in support of the visitors. Fortunately, for Susie and the three' Jays' their carer was a woman of formidable determination.

She appeared now from the booking office, with the four British passports in her hand and an anxious frown creasing her broad Slavic brow. The Russian woman made it quite clear there was no possibility of obtaining a sleeping berth to St. Petersburg that night. Four faces fell. A heavy, silent gloom settled around the hippopotamus suitcases.

The invitation letter to Pushin had not arrived until a few days before departure and there had been no time to make advanced booking to St Petersburg. It had been difficult to find someone willing to translate and reply to Dr. McClure's introductory letter from the Edinburgh school. Finally the answer came to her request for the Rainbow Tree group to visit St. Sophia's Sunday school. Susie and her companions would be most welcome to stay as guests of the Orthodox priests, the letter said, and all food and accommodation would be freely provided. This presented a wonderful opportunity, not only to visit Russia's famously beautiful city but also to make new contacts for the future.

Now the deep disappointment shown by the silent, stranded

women spoke more poignantly than words to the watching Russian. She turned abruptly and walked with purposeful strides back to the ticket booth.

Minutes later, she aroused the sombre group with a loud question, 'You have dollars?'

Too surprised and dejected to argue, the stranded travellers produced several crisp new notes out of hidden money belts. Exchanging cash in a place as public as Moscow railway station was the sort of risk best avoided, but none of the bustling crowd seemed to take any notice. Svetlana impatiently indicated to her wards they must give her more and quickly. Putting their trust in the demanding woman, a stranger to the foreigners a few hours ago, they did as they were instructed. This process was repeated twice before Svetlana at last returned from the ticket booth with a triumphant smile rounding her rosy cheeks like apples.

'Come,' she commanded.

Following their escort as meekly as school children and trundling their massive luggage behind them on tiny, inadequate wheels, the four Scots tried to keep up with the urgent pace. A train snorted impatiently, revving up its engines for immanent departure. A smartly uniformed attendant stood to attention by the open door, looking as if he had stepped off the stage of an operetta and had not had time to change. Svetlana pushed the startled travellers up the retractable stairs and the attendant hauled their cargo hastily after them slamming shut the train door. The guard's whistle blew. There was barely time to turn and wave good-bye to their fairy Godmother before she diminished into a vanishing speck and was engulfed in a puff of smoke.

Someone must have waved a magic wand. They appeared to have been given the Royal suite. The faded opulence of fringed curtains, soft romantic table lamps and plump white pillows brought to mind the tear-stained face of Anna Karenina gazing soulfully into the deeply anguished eyes of Dr. Zhivago, (or something of the sort). These addled thoughts may have been the product of exhaustion but there was no anguish to destroy the astonishing transformation of the travelling group. They may be somewhat financially impoverished but the flamboyant luxury of their overnight accommodation brought gales of laughter to shake off the tension from aching shoulders and worried faces. The sleeping car attendant delivered golden tea in tall, steaming glasses and pointed meaningfully to his watch. Did he mean they would arrive in St. Petersburg in eight hours time or eight o'clock in the morning?

'Who cares?' laughed Susie and the three 'Jay's,' sinking back into the comfort and security of the inviting bunks, imagining a horse-drawn carriage would await them and gallop through glistening snowy tracks to a white palace tucked away within the silver birch forest. The dreaming began before their heavy heads hit the crisply laundered pillows.

The sleeping women were rudely awakened with loud knocking and shouting voices. Peering blearily through the golden fringes of the curtains, they saw fully dressed passengers walking briskly past the train window. They had arrived in St. Petersburg and were still in their pyjamas. Hastily pulling on crumpled clothes and splashing cold water upon sleep-creased faces the confused passengers were hustled out onto the platform by the attendant. He was clearly annoyed by their tardiness and his muttered words probably meant something like 'bloody foreigners!'

Two round beaming faces came towards them. The younger one opened her mouth and said with a distinctly Scottish accent, 'Good morning and welcome to St. Petersburg.'

Irina, the Russian pupil of Susie's old school, and her handsome father, Anton welcomed the dishevelled group. As well as being driven to Pushkin, seven kilometres outside town, the visitors were treated to a personally conducted tour of the fabulous city on the way. It may not have been a horse-drawn carriage and there was no sign of snow upon the sun- drenched streets, but golden domes and stately palaces there were in abundance.

St. Sophia's Cathedral was a round, white building and with turreted bell tower standing beside it, looked like a newly iced wedding cake. A short distance away was a squat house in matching style and colour. This would be Susie's and the three Jay's home for the next three days. Above the main floor, where the offices of the busy church and a beautiful refectory were situated, were two double guest rooms. The four women were invited to join the resident community for breakfast as soon as they had unpacked.

Light poured through wide, tall windows of the refectory and shone upon the heavily laden table. Breakfast was a serious meal in Russia. The guests were ushered in by Irina and her benevolent father and shown to wooden chairs with high, carved backs. They did not sit down, but stood behind the chairs in the manner of their hosts. They appeared to be waiting for something, or perhaps someone?

Suddenly a procession of black-robed priests entered the refectory like a gust of wind, their long gowns sweeping majestically through the room. Hugely bearded and theatrically attired with, what looked remarkably like tea cosies on hairy heads and mayors' chains around sturdy necks, these exceptionally large men assembled themselves around the table. The rapt silence was ripped apart like curtains from a stage, and the performance began. A booming baritone filling every waiting space with a sound so amazing and prolonged that it seemed more like an operatic aria than a breakfast grace. But this was no ordinary place.

This was Russia!

Breakfast, like all the meals, was a feast, cooked in the adjoining kitchen by Lydia. This wonderful woman produced home made bread and cakes, a huge variety of fresh salads, fish, cheese, honey and caviar with unrelenting cheerfulness and skill. When they had eaten like princesses and freshened up in the adjoining showers of their bedrooms, Irina and Anton were waiting for them, eager to show the visitors the treasures of the old tsarist city.

It had a completely different atmosphere from the rural town in central Russia to which Susie had grown accustomed on her annual trips to this vast and varied country. The extravagant grandeur in the many rooms of wall to wall mosaics, floor by floor of inlaid marquetry, ceiling after ceiling of chandeliers and acres of priceless treasures assaulted the senses with unimaginable craftsmanship, wealth and talent. It was necessary to walk quietly around the landscaped parks and slightly shabby monuments, surrounding the giant palaces, in order to restore a more normal equilibrium. It was like coming out of a theatre after being swept into the realms of fantasy and walking home in refreshing rain at the end of a blistering hot day.

But the Scots hadn't come just to sightsee.

Susie was determined to create an opportunity for the members of St. Sophia's community to see the Rainbow Tree Exhibition. She had hoped and even expected that it might have been a chance to display the hangings in the Cathedral or the Sunday school, but as it was Easter week this was not possible. The children were on holiday and there were church services every day from dawn 'til dusk.

Besides there were no balconies from which to hang anything and every available space in the cathedral was highly decorated and embellished with glittering icons, numerous golden candles and intricately carved screens through which the priests popped in and out with arresting irregularity.

The stark contrast between the plain, bare interiors of most Scottish churches was echoed in the differing styles of worship. One used visual and performing arts to lift the spirits and to praise God while the other encouraged a simpler approach to the Almighty where the soul was not distracted by exterior stimulus. Unless, of course there happened to be a large and colourful exhibition of children's work exploding above the congregation!

The Rainbow Tree exploded into the deserted basement under the feet of Father Gnady's secretary as she sat unaware at the desk in the priest's office. There was nowhere else to put it and no other way of conveying the real purpose of the visit to St. Petersburg. It was their last day. Susie had declined to go on the outing to view yet more treasures and stayed behind to unpack the hidden treasure concealed in the black suitcases upstairs. When she had finished her task she knocked nervously on the office door. Father Gnady looked up in surprise as she entered the room. She walked up to the priest and simply taking him by the hand, like Svetlana, gave the quiet command,' Come.'

She led the huge, smiling, puzzled man down to the rooms where the Sunday school children had their lessons. Draped over every desk, table, chair and cupboard was a sea of creativity in all the colours of the rainbow. He stood in silent amazement. Then walking from patchwork to patchwork, touching each piece with an unconcealed awe, he saw, he understood, he felt the energy flowing out to meet him like an incoming tide. No words were needed, no explanations adequate to communicate the unspoken message in the silence. It danced like sunbeams upon the sparkling sequins and both beholders knew the little children had opened the door to the hidden treasures in each of their hearts.

Father Gnady immediately arranged for an exhibition of the Rainbow Tree, in the main hall of St Sophia's residential building in Pushkin, that afternoon. Lydia, the cook helped Susie to hang the patchworks in time for the whole community of priests, choir members, household staff and Sunday school teachers to view between three and four o'clock. June, Jane and Jo returned to find themselves thrown into an impromptu presentation of the friendship project F.I.S.H. which they hoped would continue and develop the links made by the Rainbow Tree project. Small banners, with the new logo embroidered onto them, made appropriate gifts and helped to put a seal on this promising contact.

Although it was a struggle to repack all the hangings into the suitcases before setting off to catch the overnight train back to Moscow, Susie and her gallant friends all felt the visit to St. Petersburg had been worth every effort and were sure an important link had been made for the future.

When the bedraggled quartet stumbled out of the overnight train onto the platform at Moscow's Railway Station, it seemed as if they had left it just a minute ago. St. Petersburg and the Royal Suite had already faded like a dream in the cold morning light. A haughty woman in a black leather jacket strode towards the untidy muddle of baggage, coats, carrier bags and tousled passengers. Her fur collar framed a carefully made up face and her high-heeled boots spiked the ground like exclamation marks.

'You are the Scottish group?'

It was more of a statement than a question. All four nodded in affirmation, somewhat taken aback by the disapproving glance that swept over the inordinately large amount of luggage.

'Follow please.' They followed. Their leader did not look back as she proceeded to carve her way through the crowded station, nor did she appear to have any concern for the struggling women trying to keep up with her. A young man in army uniform sprang to attention as soon as he caught sight of the figure in black leather and threw his cigarette under the car against which he was lounging. She was the general's wife. He had been hastily taken off his normal duties in the transport department to act as chauffeur to her and the foreign visitors. If he was surprised to see the dishevelled travellers he did not move a muscle to show it. The general's wife indicated to the sweating man that he should perform the impossible task of loading the luggage into the car boot. She then ensconced herself in the front passenger's seat stretching out her long boots comfortably, whilst pointing the four waiting women in the direction of the back seat. This seemed as inadequate as the boot but somehow people and baggage were finally squashed into the bulging car. The driver took his place and waited for instructions from the cool lady who spoke curtly in Russian in the manner of one used to giving orders.

The car lurched forwards, the gearbox ground noisily in the grimy hand of the army sergeant. It soon became obvious that his 'normal duties' were those of a tank driver who had little experience of driving in town. The A-Z map book of Moscow, to which he constantly referred, did nothing to accelerate their slow and painful progress. After several abortive attempts to reach Red Square, the general's wife's patience snapped. The car jolted to a halt with one wheel mounting the kerb.

The heat was swelteringly, steam rose from the bonnet and perspiration trickled down every face but that of the immaculate lady. She descended gracefully onto the pavement, indicating her passengers should do the same. They were in sight of the Kremlin, its famous silhouette dominating the skyline. It was not far to walk and certainly much quicker and cooler than pursuing the journey by car. The driver was no doubt relieved to return to the station alone, where (it was explained) he would deposit the cases and bags in the left luggage office ready to be collected before their owners boarded the train to Cheboksary.

Unfortunately or fortunately, depending on the degree of fatigue the tourists felt, the Kremlin Museums were closed. After the obligatory tour of Red Square, the fabulous new shopping mall and watching the guards change place at the War Memorial, the general's wife invited Susie and the three 'Jays' to her home to rest and repair and relax for a few hours.

She had become much friendlier while they walked and tried to converse and turned out to be a marvellous cook. The meal presented to her visitors had the hallmark of Russian hospitality and a few glasses of wine had them all laughing and toasting each other's health in no time. It was not until they returned (by taxi) to the station that a trace of her haughtiness reappeared.

Impatiently standing at the top of a steep flight of steps, the general's wife watched the four weary women heaving the heavy cases up, bump by bump. Perhaps she did not know what was inside them and imagined they were full of disproportionately large personal wardrobes. Her disdainful glance fell upon June, whose petite figure was weighed down by a rucksack and overnight bag as well as the cumbersome load on the trolley behind her. The fur coat, she had insisted on bringing, kept slipping off her arm.

The watching lady took pity, 'May I take your coat?'

It was a gesture of such stylish incongruity that it gave much cause for mirth as the overnight train to Cheboksary finally drew out of Moscow. Once again, laughter washed away the tension of the day and ensured a good night's sleep.

The station platform was crowded when the train arrived exactly on time the following morning. Susie had warned the three 'Jays' to be prepared to have their photographs taken the minute they showed their faces at the window. Precautions had been made to ensure they looked their best.

Now with curlers and night cream removed, make-up applied and fresh blouses donned, the intrepid four made their appearance before the waiting crowd. Shrieks of welcome, feverish waving and a mad dash to greet the bearers of the Rainbow Tree engulfed them in a swirling mass. Flash bulbs competed with the bright spring sunshine and burly men struggled to heave the giant cases off the train with nonchalant displays of strength. Clutching the inevitable, wilting bouquets and an assortment of hand baggage the visitors were escorted to a fleet of waiting cars.

The plan was to meet for lunch at the Beer Museum, (only Russia could have such a thing), after they had settled in with their host families. Susie, as always stayed with Yelena and 'our husband'. This rare slip in her usually perfect English, when referring in this way to her spouse, had caused the Russian teacher to say to her Scottish friend, 'We share everything!'

Nicolei enjoyed the joke and greeted his 'visiting wife' with a bone-crushing bear hug before vacating the residential marital bedroom in order to let her move in. She no longer protested at this typically generous act of unselfish hospitality and gratefully sank onto the familiar bed in her 'Russian home'.

Lunch was in a private dining room in the small Chuvashian

Museum. These people were as proud of their special identity as the Scots were of theirs. The culture was preserved and honoured in daily life and the tablecloth and napkins were wonderful examples of local embroidery. The intimate meal was the last time that the six teachers were alone with their guests in the course of the five-day Festival. The opportunity to reminisce about the Festival in Scotland launching the Millennium tour a year ago and to plan quietly for the culmination of their joint venture was a deeply thoughtful gesture on the part of the organiser.

As the friends strolled by the riverside of the swollen Volga to digest the copious amount they had just consumed, there was a lull in the balmy air, all the more sweet, because of the storm of activity about to break.

Every school was eager to receive the visitors and to impress them with their knowledge of English and the special new works made to celebrate the completion of the Rainbow Tree project. The art exhibitions were more elaborate than in previous years, the concerts more extensive, the singing more professional and the dancing more lively. Competitions were organised to express ideas and hopes for the twenty first century in all manner of written and artistic ways. Two new Trees of Life sported stuffed and embroidered fruits of amazing variety and size.

The foursome reel was a wild success, particularly when the taped music failed and the dancers had to sing as well as remember the steps! The audience obliged by clapping and joining the breathless voices in the spirit of the unusual rendering of the traditional dance to the tune of the William Tell overture.

Later in the week one of the Cumbrian teachers arrived, not only with another new 'Tree of Life' but also with a group of Morris dancers who had sensibly brought their own musicians. They added to the international flavour and made a new contribution to the cultural gathering.

The main event was to take place on Easter Sunday at the Opera

House. The vast marble foyer was used as the exhibition hall for the Rainbow Tree hangings and display of related artwork recently created by many local schools. Performing arts ensembles from all over the Republic of Chuvashia were combining to produce a celebration of 'Dances of the World' and Susie was to open proceedings with an excerpt from the 'Original Seed' drama.

The theatre director was understandably dubious when he was asked to include her traditional dance. A retired ballerina would not necessarily be able to reach the high standard he insisted upon from all the performers. She would be required to attend the dress rehearsal, he said, and he would decide then if her contribution would be suitable.

The retired ballerina warmed up in the wings along with young, talented performers and the tense atmosphere filled her limbering body with adrenalin. The director summoned the mature dancer onto the stage eyeing her neatly clad figure critically. She was still trim and supple and carried herself with professional poise. Listening carefully to his directions and marking the pattern and movements according to the placing of the opening tableau, she nodded her understanding. The director signalled to the sound gallery to play the special recording he had chosen from Shostakovitch's 'Gadfly' suite. The full orchestral force, complete with organ, brought added drama and depth to the familiar melody. Susie responded, with what, she hoped, was appropriate panache and filled the huge stage with broad sweeping movements carefully designed to follow the directions required. She had not lost the ballerina's touch. The watching man nodded his approval and the rehearsal commenced without delay.

It soon became apparent that the simple poncho, she was proposing to wear, would be inadequate. The costumes of the Opening Tableau were fabulous and ambitious, each representing the seven themes of the Rainbow Tree Exhibition. Space had a flowing cloak of celestial brilliance, Water balanced a ship in full sail upon her elaborate coiffeur, Air's translucent wings spread mightily from his arms, Earth carried a globe in the manner of Colossus, Wild Animals had spiked his hair to resemble a lion's mane and Humanity was a girl of such grace and beauty that Hope, in her shimmering red robe could only feel encouraged and inspired.

If Susie was to take her place amidst such splendour she would have to have a new costume. Time to go shopping

* * *

THE SPIRIT OF THE RAINBOW TREE

The sun shone brightly through the net curtains, the door to the balcony was open but little air flowed past the triple glazing. Easter Sunday was going to be a hot day. Susie stirred in the double bed so recently vacated in her honour by Yelena and 'our husband'. The flat was silent. No sound or movement emerged from the living room where her hostess slept on the sofa with her daughter, Natasha. The son's tiny box room, opposite the only bathroom, had its door tightly closed.

Susie tiptoed to the kitchen to make herself a cup of black tea, (milk was not a Russian habit), and took it back to the silent sanctuary of the bedroom. The golden brocade that she had bought yesterday was spread out upon a chair. It had not been difficult to find something suitable for her costume as the town was well stocked with fabric shops. But the material was more beautiful than she imagined. It was perfect. Nothing could be better suited for a golden robe for the Festival.

The dancer laid the shimmering mass upon the bed and reached for her scissors. She took a deep breath, closed her eyes and said a silent prayer. This was her prayer. The whole day would be a series of prayers. The first one was a dedication of the Easter robe she was about to create.

With one decisive stroke she slashed an opening at the top of the folded material. Putting her head through the slit, Susie took a critical look at her reflection in the wardrobe mirror. Perfect again. It was going to be a blessed day. The next task was to trim six inches off the bottom. This would make the golden gown exactly the right length as well as providing a wide binding for the deep V neckline.

It was only half past seven. For the next two hours she sat and sewed. This was the part she enjoyed. Hand sewing had always brought a sense of calm to balance the times of hectic activity. She thought of the gentle repetitive task as a form of meditation.

She meditated upon the events that had led to this day with a profound thankfulness. The Rainbow Tree had reached its destination. This particular time and place was the point to which the past eleven years of her life had been directed until this moment. This was, (as the poet said), 'the still point in a turning world where the dance is'. The dance was within her now, waiting to become visible that afternoon.

The silence broke. Yelena knocked on the bedroom door and informed Susie that she was about to leave for the Opera House. The Exhibition would be open to the public from noon and the performance would begin an hour later. A car would collect Susie at eleven. As co-ordinator of the event, she would go on ahead as there was still a great deal requiring her attention. The co-ordinator of last year's event sympathised but sent up another little prayer of gratitude that it was not her responsibility this time. Her Russian colleague was dynamic, determined, charming and efficient. Everything would be perfect.

Susie felt like Royalty as the driver offered his hand to help her extract the billowing folds of gold from the shabby car, she was no longer a Princess, she was a Queen. Entering the marble hall, a buzz of excitement greeted her. Every eye turned towards the ballerina artist whose vision had come true this day.

This was Easter Day.

The Rainbow Tree hangings seemed to rise above their material reality. Textiles, threads, beads and appliqué sang with the Spirit of Creativity and danced with childish joy. The new Trees of Life were the central focus, lit by a magnificent chandelier that sparkled like a cluster of raindrops in the sun. A rainbow of light flooded through enormous windows and shone a blessing upon the assembled works.

The performance was about to begin.

The curtain concealed the opening tableau of still silent figures, their glorious costumes crowned by the golden robe in the centre. In front of the heavy, red velvet drapes a children's choir sang the Easter hymn.

'CHRIST IS RISEN, HE IS RISEN INDEED,' the high, clear voices announced.

The red, velvet curtain slowly rose from the ground. A gasp gripped the audience. The music began. The golden dancer lifted her arms, she raised her head, her eyes glistened and the dance poured forth like a prayer. One by one she touched the wondrous creatures of the Rainbow Tree. They came alive at her silent command. The whole stage came to life. It seemed as if the lonely seed, which had fallen to the ground, had indeed multiplied and given birth to new growth.

There was no end to the dancing.

Long after the amazing celebration was over the dance continued. Long after the golden robe was packed away in the suitcase the gold glittered, long after the music stopped, the movement sang.

The words of one little girl capture the spirit of the Rainbow Tree. When she first saw it tumbling out of its bag like a plant erupting from the broken husk of a seed, she burst out,

'Come and see, come quickly and see.'

Susie came.

Then children came running from every corner. They gathered round the huge patchwork lifting it up and down like a parachute.

Its branches began to dance with colour and light and the little girl cried, 'COME AND SEE, THE TREE IS ALIVE!

And they all saw what Susie had seen when the Indian children gave her back the key to her whole life over twelve years ago.

And now she knows that the light of the Rainbow Tree is living within her own true self.

Chapter Twenty Two

THE TREASURE AT THE END OF THE RAINBOW TREE

The story of the Rainbow Tree is finished and the woman in the sunny box has gone. Her task is done but the next chapter of my life is just beginning. It is always beginning. I used to long for a happy ending but now I know there is no end to the changing seasons of my life. My journey of transformation may be completed but I am still growing. Like a tree I need to stay still and put down roots.

After four years here I feel I have taken root in my native soil and I am flourishing.

I had no difficulty in letting go of the Rainbow Tree after the final festival in Russia a year ago. The hangings have been widely exhibited and we hope they will go on to travel further and inspire new developments. The foundations for future friendships and exchange visits have been firmly laid. Already the work, started by me in 1993, has been taken up by the three Jay's and others since the F.I.S.H. mission in Easter 2001, but the Rainbow Tree Exhibition is still freely available and open to new initiatives.

I am deeply grateful for all the Rainbow Tree has taught and given to me. If it had not been for the international textile project my story would be of no particular interest or value. The light it has shone upon my journey gave me a sense of direction and showed me the way when I was lost in the 'cloud of unknowing'. I had to have something beyond myself to strive towards. I could give no service to the planet, the community, the poor or the rich until my ego was shattered. Every time it reared its ugly head something happened, and will continue to happen, to bring me back to the ground of humility.

I have learned all the gifts God has bestowed upon me are worth nothing if they are not given back to His glory. I am nothing if I am not a vehicle, a channel, a vessel in which the Spirit of Life may live and love and dance and be.

Mostly I am just letting Life live me these days. I have discovered a deep contentment resting, not in having much, but in coveting little. I am at home with myself and my needs are simple. I have grown to love solitude, silence and space. I have no need of another project to give my life meaning or purpose because I have reached a place where I can be alone and at peace with myself. This is the hidden treasure now revealed at the end of the Rainbow Tree.

I am no longer afraid of growing old on my own; I shall grow old gracefully in 'a condition of complete simplicity which costs not less than everything' and gives back all that was lost.

My state of grace is a lovely place. I can only enter it when I am at peace with myself. When I am me. This state of detachment from concern and emotion creates a space where all the parts I have played come together and become one. I am all one when I am alone in the lovely place I have discovered. It is like a well of silence where I can drink my fill. It fills me with quiet waters circulating my head and heart and whole body with a new rhythm. It is deeper, slower, steadier and stronger than before and it breathes in me like a whispering voice telling me who I am.

I am learning new arts; the art of listening and waiting, of homemaking and gardening but above all, the art of loving. Loving from a distance.

I think of my son and my daughter. Love has held us together and woven an unbreakable thread between us even when we have tried to detach ourselves from each other. Love has refused to let us go. Although I shall always be sad that the conditions did not prevail for the bud of love to grow between their father and me, I am glad that I am sad. It means love is still alive in the bulb of my crocus of hope.

I give thanks for the love which links father and mother through son and daughter and for the freedom allowing it to flow and grow in the distance between us.

Love absorbs my hopes; love absolves my regrets; love dissolves my hurts and transforms all distance and space into one eternal embrace.

My son and my daughter have both come to visit me here. They have said, 'we have seen you in your place and now we know why you are here.'

It is my home.

When I knew they were coming, I felt love flooding into me long before they were here and after they had left I wrote,

'Now that you have seen me in my place
And you know where I am,
I can be fully here.
Now your presence is always with me
Living in me here
And I am no longer alone.
Now when you remember me and see me
In the eye of your mind
We are held together in love.

I love being here all the time. Even in the depths of winter when the light is long in coming and short in staying. I love to lie in bed in the cold, dark mornings and wait for the light to come. I wait in silence, in stillness and in the dark. I draw back the curtains and light a solitary candle, place it on the windowsill and creep back into bed to wait.

There is nothing to see but darkness. It is solid. Not like the thin dusk barely veiling the sky in summer. No shapes, no colours, no movement show through the deep indigo panes.

I wait. The black shroud, concealing all life, will disperse. Even now there is a slight, dim indistinct line between a lighter and a deeper darkness. Tones of colour begin to divide indigo from blue-black navy. The distant fir-clad hill is still draped in an all- consuming disguise, extinguishing blue-green and grass-green and tall, proud trees on undulating slopes.

The sky is heavy with motionless weight, suppressing daylight for another hour. The time has not yet come. Even light must wait upon God. The light of the world is not yet here but it is coming, always coming. It comes nearer and nearer until, at last near becomes here.

And now it is Easter again. The light is abundantly here. The sun shone early this morning and clothed my soul in a golden robe of radiant new energy. Everything around me dances to the song of spring. All the dead, bare branches on the sleeping trees awake with colour and burst into being. I live in the light of the Rainbow Tree. The original patchwork has faded and died but the life of the tree lives on in me.

As a tree breathes in air and light,
So I breathe.
As a tree drinks in water and life,
So I drink.
As the leaves grow green and dance in the wind,
So I grow, so I dance, so I live.
As a tree puts down roots in the earth,
So I do.
As a tree takes shape and gains strength,
So I stand.
As a tree bears fruit and gives from itself
So I rejoice and am glad and give thanks.
Now the way of the tree has healed me
And I see
The truth of the tree has freed me
And I know
The spirit of life held in each tiny seed
Dwells in me as I am
Here and now.

Cover and Layout: Stephen M.L. Young
                    Elgin
                    Scotland
                    itsmybook@aol.com

Font: Adobe Garamond (11pt)

Copies of this book can be ordered via the Internet:
                    www.librario.com
or from:
                    Librario Publishing Ltd
                    Brough House
                    Milton Brodie
                    Kinloss
                    Moray IV36 2UA
                    Tel /Fax No 01343 850 617